NEW DIRECTIONS FOR ADULT AND CONTINUING EDUCATION

Ralph G. Brockett, *University of Tennessee, Knoxville*
EDITOR-IN-CHIEF

Alan B. Knox, *University of Wisconsin, Madison*
CONSULTING EDITOR

Professionals' Ways of Knowing: New Findings on How to Improve Professional Education

H. K. Morris Baskett
University of Calgary, Alberta, Canada

Victoria J. Marsick
Teachers College, Columbia University

EDITORS

Number 55, Fall 1992

JOSSEY-BASS PUBLISHERS
San Francisco

27292012

LC
5251
.N48
no.55

PROFESSIONALS' WAYS OF KNOWING: NEW FINDINGS ON HOW TO
IMPROVE PROFESSIONAL EDUCATION
H. K. Morris Baskett, Victoria J. Marsick (eds.)
New Directions for Adult and Continuing Education, no. 55
Ralph G. Brockett, Editor-in-Chief
Alan B. Knox, Consulting Editor

© 1992 by Jossey-Bass Inc., Publishers. All rights reserved.

No part of this issue may be reproduced in any form—except for a brief
quotation (not to exceed 500 words) in a review or professional work—
without permission in writing from the publishers.

Microfilm copies of issues and articles are available in 16mm and 35mm,
as well as microfiche in 105mm, through University Microfilms Inc., 300
North Zeeb Road, Ann Arbor, Michigan 48106.

LC 85-644750   ISSN 0195-2242   ISBN 1-55542-728-6

NEW DIRECTIONS FOR ADULT AND CONTINUING EDUCATION is part of The
Jossey-Bass Higher and Adult Education Series and is published quarterly
by Jossey-Bass Inc., Publishers, 350 Sansome Street, San Francisco, Califor-
nia 94104-1310 (publication number USPS 493-930). Second-class postage
paid at San Francisco, California, and at additional mailing offices. POST-
MASTER: Send address changes to New Directions for Adult and Continuing
Education, Jossey-Bass Inc., Publishers, 350 Sansome Street, San Francisco,
California 94104-1310.

SUBSCRIPTIONS for 1992 cost $45.00 for individuals and $60.00 for institutions, agencies, and libraries.

EDITORIAL CORRESPONDENCE should be sent to the Editor-in-Chief,
Ralph G. Brockett, Dept. of Technological and Adult Education, University
of Tennessee, 402 Claxton Addition, Knoxville, Tennessee 37996-3400.

The paper used in this journal is acid-free and meets the strictest
guidelines in the United States for recycled paper (50 percent
recycled waste, including 10 percent post-consumer waste).
Manufactured in the United States of America.

Contents

93 0108
CARLOW COLLEGE, GREENE PA

EDITORS' NOTES

When sixty researchers and continuing professional educators gathered at the concluding meeting of the three-day conference Professionals' Ways of Knowing, held in the fall of 1991 in Montreal, Quebec, Canada, it was apparent that something unusual had happened. Four cluster groups had shared their research and informed views about how professionals learn and change and had collectively tried in their own way to advance their understanding of the continuing professional education field. Now they were coming to tell their co-conferees about what had happened to them in the conference.

One group described their experience with the metaphor of constructing a house or building. Michael Price, one of the group participants, described his group's understanding about professional learning and change this way: "Once constructed, a house is not easily abandoned or remodeled. We may take vacations to other houses or settings, and in doing so gain new insights; but to effect permanent change in practice we must make changes to the structures or mechanisms themselves. These changes are usually small, like rearranging the furniture or redecorating. Sometimes, we may add a room or knock out a wall. Under extreme conditions, we may *transform* our 'home' into something entirely different—usually a result of a catastrophe, such as a fire, or getting fired."

The group explained that each of us as professionals builds a house of the mind. Learning is like energy, and the house is built to control the flow of that energy. Some energy is kept out, some let in, and some brought in mechanically. We "insulate" against the environment, and we provide windows to obtain desired views. Our professional life is another house in which we live. In order to see problems, we may have to remove ourselves from our houses, to get a view from another house, or from a new location.

The conference was much like that metaphor. People who were involved in the study and practice of continuing professional education (CPE) were stepping outside to get a glimpse at what was happening outside of their areas of expertise and, in so doing, were open to new ways of seeing and understanding professional learning and change.

This volume, *Professionals' Ways of Knowing,* attempts to continue the spirit of the conference—to break out of our traditional ways of thinking and acting and to seek new structures and frameworks in order to see what has changed while we have been locked in our profession-imposed houses.

The conference title attracted like-minded people because it reflected the growing discomfort with the old lenses through which we have been seeing and studying professional learning. Mechanistic, linear, and rationalistic perspectives, while portraying one view of reality, only tell part of the story. People came because the conference call for papers had promised a mutual exploration rather than a rain of words. They were attracted because they knew that there were other ways of seeing and understanding professional learning and change, but there was presently neither language nor frameworks to give legitimacy to their thoughts.

Most of the work in this volume derives from that conference, although each author has made extensive revisions and some authors have contributed work not presented at the conference. From the original thirty-three presentations and keynote addresses, the chapters here were selected because they reflect the freshness and breadth of thought current in the field of continuing professional education and at the same time meet the need of the practitioner for concrete, useful, topical, and timely ideas.

We regret that editorial dictates forced us to select only a few of the conference papers and to portray only a limited number of professional groups. The reader may wish to obtain a copy of the full proceedings, *Professionals' Ways of Knowing and the Implications for CPE* (1991).

Professionals' Ways of Knowing?

The expression "professionals' ways of knowing" may seem to be unnecessary jargon. In daily usage, the term *knowledge* has come to refer to something that is static, acquired, or stored, just as one puts away groceries for future use. This definition is not in keeping with how we now understand the concept of knowledge. In light of our own experience and research, we offer our understanding of the following ideas and their importance.

Ways of Knowing. This phrase conveys something much more dynamic than the manner in which the term knowledge is used today. "Ways of knowing" suggests that learning is something in process and that it involves a continuous cycle of moving to greater certainty on a variety of issues, actions, and agendas. Belenky, Clinchy, Goldberger, and Tarule (1986) use the term *ways of knowing* to indicate that there is something other than *received knowledge,* that learners (specifically, women in their study) make unique sense out of their experiences and that people can be active in creating new (for them) understandings and hence knowledge. Ways of knowing also conveys something less absolute and more pluralistic than does the term knowledge, and this characterization is more in tune with what we now know about learning and professional change.

Professional. Jarvis (1983, p. 27) tells us that "the professional is one who continually seeks the mastery of the branch of learning upon which his occupation is based, so that he may offer a service to his client." He also reports that there appears to be a general consensus that "at the foundation of every occupation claiming professional status is knowledge and its application" (p. 19). A high degree of independent judgment, based on a collective, learned body of ideas, perspectives, information, norms, and habits is also involved in professional knowing. Generally, this judgment is used to serve other individuals and groups rather than one's own self-interest.

The phenomenal increase in the knowledge base that characterizes our Western technological and information-oriented society has resulted in a range of new professionalizing occupations, such as computer experts, space technologists, and human resources development specialists. This expansion has blurred the distinction between occupations that can be regarded as professional and those that cannot.

Learning. Lately, there has been a tendency in the literature to use the words *learning* and *education* interchangeably. We see them as quite different. Learning is a personal, emotional, and cognitive act, the results of which are unique to the individual. We all learn all of the time, but no two individuals learn exactly the same thing from a similar experience. We define learning as "the ways in which individuals or groups acquire, interpret, reorganize, change, assimilate, or apply related clusters of information, skills, and feelings. Learning is primary to the way in which people construct meaning in their personal and shared organizational lives" (Marsick, 1987, p. 4). Although learning is unique to the individual or group, others may try to shape and influence that learning. Any deliberate, planned effort to do so is what we call education.

Purpose and Organization of This Volume

The goal of this volume is to challenge and inform those involved in the development and training of professionals. We hope that readers will reflect on the tensions between what we are now coming to know about professional learning and change and the way in which much professional education is carried out. We hope also that readers will address these issues in their own practice, and that they will use the alternate perspectives and ideas here in their quests to improve the education and training of professionals.

In Chapter One, we begin with the premise that the field's present understanding of how professionals learn and change is out of whack with the findings of recent research, which has resulted in a gap between practice and theory. We review some of that research and speculate on its implications for the practice of CPE.

In the following four chapters, the authors offer concrete and practical ways in which professionals and CPE practitioners can respond to the growing understanding of professional learning. In Chapter Two, Klevans, Smutz, Shuman, and Bershad examine an issue of great importance to professional associations and regulatory bodies concerned with maintaining professionwide minimum standards of competence: how to help professionals identify and learn what they do not know. The authors' systematic reporting on how they developed and tested a competence-based, self-diagnostic tool for architects to use in maintaining their professional competence offers clear possibilities for other professions that are able to establish a foundation of professional knowledge on which their members must practice. This approach also offers promise to those who find mandatory continuing education too problematic a tool for maintaining professional competence. The learning and motivational effects of undergoing the self-assessment process also hold considerable promise for continuing professional development.

In Chapter Three, Jennett and Pearson describe a range of practice-based approaches used recently in medicine to facilitate medical practitioners' learning and understanding. From face-to-face peer support systems to learning to access data bases for real-time problem solving, the possibilities and limitations of these methods are examined.

Based on data from interviews of 450 professionals, Farmer, Buckmaster, and LeGrand, in Chapter Four, explain the approach that they developed to enable learning of ill-defined, complex, high-risk technical tasks. Cognitive apprenticeship offers one of the clearest technologies at a satisfactory level of specificity to deal with such tasks. Many professions, from engineering to nursing, will find the level of prescription, based on broad experience, both comforting and helpful.

In Chapter Five, Ellerington, Marsick, and Dechant explore relatively untouched areas of professional learning and change. Human resources developers are not traditionally thought of as professionals, yet they function much in the fashion of corporate lawyers or accountants. Their client is the organization rather than the individual. The notion of capability development, as discussed by the authors, adds a useful new dimension. It connects a set of professional competencies with the organization's goals and, in so doing, acknowledges the realities of the organizational context in which many professionals operate today.

Until recently, there has been very little investigation into how peers help each other to learn. Lovin's study, in Chapter Six, of how paramedics learn to partner, and learn from partners, offers considerable insight into this heretofore shadowy phenomenon. She also helps to demystify this area by discussing the cycle of learning that occurs in the context of practice, and the types of partnerships that most effectively facilitate on-the-job learning.

Boreham, in Chapter Seven, discusses implicit knowledge, an area about which there has been little attention paid until recently, most probably because of the difficulty of acknowledging something so ethereal in a rationally driven profession such as medicine. Although the setting is medical practice, implicit knowing occurs in all professions. Boreham unravels the mysteries of this type of knowing and examines it in a scientific context. We hope that, in so doing, he encourages all professional educators to be courageous in investigating and understanding the implications of implicit knowing for their own professions and for professional education.

Drawing from two studies of women's learning and from the literature, Loughlin and Mott, in Chapter Eight, explore the contribution that an awareness of women's learning models can make to continuing professional education practice. They conclude that professional learning can be made more meaningful if professional educators help learners to center their knowing within their authentic selves, facilitate the development of a connected and experientially focused language within the learning process, and create a context of relatedness among learners.

Moving to a broader context, Jarvis and Knox, in their respective chapters, address two important issues that span all professions: the learning of practical knowledge and the international and cultural contexts of professional knowledge. Practical knowledge has moved to the forefront of discussion and legitimacy in many professions. Previously associated with "unprofessionalism," the unearthing of practical knowledge has lent new legitimacy to what professionals have always known—many aspects of practice are not taught in professional training. In Chapter Nine, Jarvis's general treatise on practical knowledge provides a wide lens with which to view the chapters of Boreham and of Farmer, Buckmaster, and LeGrand.

In Chapter Ten, Knox explores the cultural and international dimensions and implications of professional learning. As he points out, much of the literature produced to date reflects a Western cultural bias in reference to professional learning and change. It is instructive to understand this bias, and to acknowledge that what continuing professional educators in North America perceive as acceptable ways of knowing will not necessarily be shared with their Chinese or Middle Eastern counterparts, let alone European or Native American colleagues. Clearly, this cross-cultural dimension is an important new frontier in understanding professionals' ways of knowing.

In the final chapter, Ronald M. Cervero joins us to help examine the future prospects, opportunities, and problems in the exploration of professional learning and change and in the facilitation of effective professional practice.

This volume is truly a collective effort, and we are indebted to all of the conference participants for helping us to view ways of knowing through a multitude of lenses and for encouraging us all to explore further this important field. We especially thank Louise Campbell of the University of Calgary, who so ably handled the word processing and coordination of the manuscripts for this volume. We affectionately salute Anne and Peter, our respective partners, for their caring support and help throughout the process. It is our hope that readers will find this volume instrumental in expanding their own professional ways of knowing.

H. K. Morris Baskett
Victoria J. Marsick
Editors

References

Belenky, M. F., Clinchy, B. M., Goldberger, N. R., and Tarule, J. M. *Women's Ways of Knowing: The Development of Self, Voice, and Mind.* New York: Basic Books, 1986.
Jarvis, P. *Professional Education.* London, England: Croom-Helm, 1983.
Marsick, V. J. "Introduction." In V. J. Marsick (ed.), *Learning in the Workplace.* London, England: Croom-Helm, 1987.
Professionals' Ways of Knowing and the Implications for CPE. Preconference proceedings of the Commission for Continuing Professional Education of the American Association for Adult and Continuing Education. Montreal, Quebec, Canada: Commission for Continuing Professional Education, American Association for Adult and Continuing Education, 1991. (ED 339 848)

H. K. MORRIS BASKETT is professor and program director, Faculty of Continuing Education, University of Calgary, Alberta, Canada. Much of his research, writing, and teaching as well as his professional activities have been in the field of continuing professional education and human resources development.

VICTORIA J. MARSICK is associate professor of adult and continuing education at Teachers College, Columbia University in New York City. As a specialist in action learning for management development, she is a founding member of the Institute for Leadership in International Management. She currently consults with both the private and public sectors on the design of learning organizations and training approaches.

*We are experiencing a revolution in our understanding of the role of
professionals and of professional learning and change. These
upheavals are influencing the way in which professional education
is construed and the way in which those involved in continuing
professional education need to define and carry out their business.*

Confronting New Understandings
About Professional Learning
and Change

H. K. Morris Baskett, Victoria J. Marsick

Profession bashing is almost as rampant today as Japan bashing. Discontent
with professionals—their role in today's society, their ethical judgments,
their education and training—is not new. In this chapter, we look briefly at
the questions being raised about professionals, and the challenge that these
questions pose to continuing professional educators. We then examine
recent research on professional learning and the implications of these studies for our understanding and facilitation of professional learning and change.

Changing Role of Professionals

Professions are subjected to an increasing array of pressures in today's
turbulent society. This is also true for the nonprofessions, but professionals have held a privileged, almost sacred, role in society. Professionals are
"supposed to be" more knowledgeable, ethical, socially oriented, and
independent in their judgments than are nonprofessionals. It may or may
not be fair to ask more of professionals, but society does so.

   Another wrinkle in professional education today is that North America
and Europe are information societies. A large number of people are still
illiterate and undereducated, but education has increasingly been available to a larger number of people worldwide. Along with education has
come a plethora of specialized knowledge bases that drive people in
many job categories more and more toward a professionalization of sorts.
Human resources developers, for example, need specialized education

and training, are called on to exercise judgment in ambiguous circumstances, must frequently work autonomously, and are members of vast professional networks that attempt in some way to standardize knowledge and monitor their members. Even secretaries might argue that they exercise judgment, function autonomously, and have built a specialized knowledge base. Hence, many clusters of knowledge workers identify themselves as professionals—or, at least, as paraprofessionals—and seek both status and the formation of a professional knowledge base with which members are familiar.

The demands on continuing professional educators in the 1990s have risen dramatically. A major response to those demands has been a shift to competence models. Competencies are identified by subject matter experts and clients, validated, and used as the basis for assessment and for classroom-oriented or alternative self-directed learning activities. There are several advantages of this model, not the least of which is a concern for what professionals can do, not just what they know. Moreover, alternative self-directed delivery models can be used to help people learn because success is measured by results, not by hours spent in the classroom.

Nowlen (1990, p. 20), however, has severely critiqued the competence model: "The most serious flaw in the competence approach is its underlying assumption that performance is an *individual* affair" (italics added). Nowlen represents an emerging school of thought that emphasizes an understanding of professionals in relationship to the complex environments in which they practice. Professionals do not work solo but are part of an "ensemble" that involves relationships with peers, the organization through which service is delivered, paraprofessionals on whom the professional depends to meet client needs, legislation, community concerns, and professional associations, to name but a few components. Competence is much more than an abstract set of knowledge and skills: "how things go in any one of the cultures that holds an adult is likely to influence adult functioning in other holding cultures" (p. 21) with respect to the professional and his or her interactions with clients.

Nowlen's thinking is in accord with a trend in society of acknowledging interrelationships and realizing that parts of societal units are interconnected with one another. Actions taken in one part of a unit have dramatic effects on the rest of the unit, whether the unit is a family, a community, an organization, an institution, or a social structure. This viewpoint has striking implications for both what it is that professionals need to learn as well as how they learn. The next section of this chapter explores some of these implications.

New Understandings about Learning and Change

In the past two decades there has been a virtual revolution in the way in which we have come to understand and study adult learning. Up to the late 1970s, the study of learning was primarily the domain of psychology and mostly focused on formal learning. With the impetus given by such seminal documents as *Learning to Be* (Faure, 1972), *Continuing Learning in the Professions* (Houle, 1980), and *The Reflective Practitioner* (Schön, 1983), the focus shifted from educational interventions to an understanding of learning from the learner's perspective. Early studies pointed to the gap between how and what people actually learned and how and what they said that they learned, or how and what academics thought that they learned (Argyris, 1977; Boud and Griffin, 1987; Burgoyne and Hodgson, 1983; Davies and Easterby-Smith, 1984). Progress in understanding how professionals learn has occurred on several fronts.

Where Learning Occurs. Studies of learning patterns of professionals have shown that, by and large, formally arranged continuing professional education (CPE) programs are used much less than is self-directed and self-planned learning (Tough, 1971; McCatty, 1975; Rymell, 1981; Zemke, 1985; Curry and Putnam, 1981; Matthias, 1991). Tough (1971), who was a pioneer in the move to focus on the learner, studied the contexts in which adults learned. He found that most adult learning occurred outside of formal educational systems, and that numerous learning projects were undertaken yearly by professionals. Tough's work laid the foundation for a rash of studies into adults' learning projects, and many of them focused on the arenas in which professionals learn. For example, in a study of professional men, McCatty (1975) found that 55 percent of their learning projects were work-directed, and 76 percent were self-planned. Rymell (1981) found that almost half of engineers' learning projects were vocational in nature, and 67 percent of these took place at the engineer's place of employment. Tough (1978), in a summary of learning projects studies, concluded that teachers' major learning projects are largely self-planned. Reading was stated by an overwhelming majority of a sample of male engineers, pharmacists, and physicians as the means of keeping current (Matthias, 1991).

Social Context. Much of Tough's work focuses primarily on the individual. The social context is taken into account primarily in terms of the way in which people and the environment are used as resources for learning. Spear and Mocker (1984) emphasized the environmental context in their elaboration of self-directed learning. However, most theories of self-directed learning are still focused on an individual's goals. Less attention is paid to the way in which people interact collectively within a social context. In such cases, the culture of the social unit has a strong influence on learning. Moreover, as Dechant (1989) and Marsick (1990) found in separate studies of managers, individuals often involve others in a joint learning process that is very different from self-directed learning. Collective learning occurs as groups of people engage in a collective learning project that is often initiated, and surely shaped, by the culture of the organization.

Many professionals today work within organizations. Their interaction with the social context often results in conflicts because organizations are typically directive whereas professionals enjoy considerable autonomy (Benveniste, 1987; Miller, 1986; Raelin, 1985). They are also being pushed to learn collectively, in teams, across functional boundaries because Total Quality Management demands more of this kind of interaction in order to achieve a customer-oriented, systems-perspective way of doing business. New ways of understanding team-centered professional learning in this sociocultural context are germane to this challenge.

Practical Versus Formal Knowledge. Only in the past decade or so have we begun to closely examine the concept of practical knowledge (Lave, 1988; Sternberg and Wagner, 1986). Schön (1983) pointed out that universities that train professionals are devoted to one particular approach to knowledge and ignore other kinds of knowledge that professionals demonstrate, such as practical competence and professional artistry. Professionals, he stated, "exhibit a kind of knowing-in-practice, most of which is tacit" (1983, p. viii). Rather than operating in situations in which they can draw on the technical and rational knowledge learned in universities, which assumes predictability and control of the environment, professionals function in a world "characterized by uncertainty, disorder, and indeterminacy" (p. 16). There are no universal rules, as taught by professional schools, to apply in these situations, and professionals use reflection-in-action and reflection-on-action to deal with most situations confronted by professionals.

Most professionals and professional educators know implicitly that there is a gap between what is taught in universities and what is needed in practice in the real world. Calderhead (1990) in teaching and Benner (1984) in nursing have been among those who have addressed this issue in the literature. In effect, Schön and others who support his line of argument have encouraged those who knew that there were other "ways of knowing," though there was neither a language to express nor even acknowledgment that these "other realities" were real and legitimate.

Kinds of Knowledge. Not only have we begun to realize that much professional knowledge is of a practical kind, but recent studies suggest that there are many different kinds of knowledge. Eraut (1988), for example, suggests that school administrators have six different kinds of knowledge: knowledge of people, situational knowledge, knowledge of educational practice, conceptual knowledge, process knowledge, and control knowledge. In a field study of social workers, Baskett (1983) found that these professionals used six different kinds of knowledge, only one of which was formally taught in university schools of social work. In studying nurses, Benner (1984) found that their practical knowledge or know-how consisted of seven domains and several competencies.

Using a somewhat different schema, Mezirow (1981) has suggested that there are at least three different types of knowledge: instrumental, dialogic, and self-reflective.

Fox, Mazmanian, and Putnam (1989) noted that physicians learned in two different ways—experientially, while doing something, and deliberatively, through thinking, reading, and reflecting—and that each strategy dominated about half the time. Baskett (1983) found that the social workers in his study tended to have two different strategies, and these were linked to the nature of the task. When not pushed for immediate action, social work practitioners scanned their environments using print and formal knowledge. However, when they needed to act immediately, they used a much more limited repertoire, drawing on previous experiences, consulting with peers, supervisors, and clients, and referring to manuals.

Research and opinion now suggest that knowledge as taught formally in professional schools is really just the tip of the "knowledge iceberg," and that the other nine-tenths of professional practice knowledge has been heretofore unseen and unheralded. Up until very recently, most postqualifying education or CPE has concentrated on the tip of the iceberg. Knowledge embedded in practice, while always used by professionals, is only now beginning to be understood. Is it any wonder that employers of newly graduated professionals have complained that they are not trained to work in the real world?

Where Knowledge Comes From. Conventional understanding has it that knowledge comes from somewhere—books, journals, lectures, tapes—that this knowledge can be stored for future consumption. This mechanistic model has dominated most of the educational world's behavior until very recently. It is now realized that this model is primarily associated with one particular kind of knowledge, namely, formal knowledge.

A more recent view is that knowledge is actually created by people in interaction with their environment (Hunt, 1987; Boud and Griffin, 1987). This view suggests that although there is "knowledge" that is accumulated, "knowing" is personal and involves gaining closer and closer approximations of a sense of certainty. In this process, professionals constantly engage in a kind of dialogue with themselves and their environment and constantly revisit the myriad issues and problems with which they are grappling at any one time (Schön, 1983; Baskett, 1991). For example, even though a lawyer may know about a past case, she or he "knows" something new only when the old case is seen as relevant to and useful for purposes of the present case. Up to that point, knowledge about the past case was indeed simply stored information.

Resources for Learning. Research into the resources used by professionals in learning shows that books, journals, and courses constitute only one portion. Most professional learning occurs in interaction with everyday work problems and usually involves a number of sources (Zemke, 1985).

In a study of changes in the practice behavior of physicians, Geertsma, Parker, and Whitbourne (1982) identified six "agencies of change": colleagues, journals, conferences, continuing medical education programs, drug company representatives, and patients. Journals and colleague communication were by far the most frequent agencies involved in two of the change stages identified. Baskett (1983) found that social workers used up to seven different sources when involved in gaining certainty about their practice strategies. There was considerable overlap between the sources or agencies found in these two studies.

These and other studies suggest that there is a dynamic interaction between the learner and the environment, and that various resources are used in an unconscious way as the professional attempts to confront everyday work concerns. We have much yet to learn about these interactions and the role that external resources play in forming professional understanding.

Cycle of Learning. Another conventional wisdom that continues to dominate education is the idea that professional judgment or knowing involves an instant digestion of ideas, facts, and attitudes, which are then imported into practice. Various conferences and workshops for professionals operate primarily on the idea that once information or ideas are received and understood, there will be an automatic transfer to workplace situations. Studies suggest that the process of becoming "knowledgeable" is long, circuitous, and far more circumscribed and holistic than previously imagined.

Fox, Maxmanian, and Putnam (1989) found changes in physicians to be of four different kinds, some of them very complex, involving personal and environmental factors, and sometimes taking many years to complete. Geertsma, Parker, and Whitbourne (1982) identified a cycle of change involving priming, focusing, and follow-up. These and other studies suggest that formal educational programs are only one small part of the overall learning and change process of professionals, and that the professional learning and change is so complex that conventional approaches to professional training need to be rethought.

Impact of Continuing Professional Education. One reason we as educators of professionals need to rethink what we are doing, and how we may do it, is that, as the evidence suggests, the present way we are doing business is not always working. The number of studies of the effectiveness of CPE has grown considerably, but the evidence as to whether training and education of professionals makes a difference is very mixed (Knox, 1979).

Fox, Maxmanian, and Putnam (1989) reviewed the literature on continuing medical education and concluded that the issues were far more complex than previously thought, and that many variables effecting change in physician behavior had not been accounted for and were difficult to control in impact studies. Guskey (1986) advised that studies into the impact on teacher competence of staff development have noted its general lack of effectiveness.

These data are not terribly helpful to continuing professional educators who want to improve their effectiveness because the information provides no indications about how they should change their practice. What Knox (1979) and Fox, Mazmanian, and Putnam (1989) have done is to challenge the very assumption that education is the answer to making a difference. Researchers such as Cervero, Azzaretto, and Tallman (1990) state that it is more fruitful to pay attention to how practitioners actually learn and change, rather than to assume a direct effect of education on practitioner behavior and try to test effectiveness on this assumption. The former is the direction taken by many of the authors in this volume.

Conclusion

The above discussion suggests that we are experiencing a revolution in our understanding of professional learning and change and of the ways in which we can study this phenomenon. The growing acceptance of interpretive and critical perspectives as legitimate additions to the study of individual and social phenomena has allowed for a more holistic examination of professional learning and change. But when one is in the midst of tumultuous change, it is very difficult to fully grasp the significance and meaning of these new viewpoints. At this time, we can only speculate on their implications for how continuing professional educators may more effectively achieve the goal of wise professional practice.

The authors of this volume seek to reframe the questions of CPE. A story told by W. E. Deming illustrates the need for reframing. Some U.S. automobile executives were comparing the quality of the critical elements of their engines and of those made by the Japanese. The woman doing the testing found that each of the many engine rings made in Japan reached the exact same point on her testing instrument. After numerous trials with the same result, she became puzzled and complained to her supervisor: "My testing instrument must be broken!" She never considered that, unlike the U.S. experience, the Japanese rings could be and were all made exactly to specification!

Reframing is powerful. Even if it does not leave us with all of the answers, it does help us to ask new questions. A focus on learning and the learner in CPE, rather than on education, opens us to new questions, some of which are explored in the chapters that follow.

References

Argyris, C. "Double Loop Learning in Organizations." *Harvard Business Review*, 1977, 55 (5), 115–125.

Baskett, H.K.M. "Continuing Professional Education in Social Work: An Examination of Knowledge Utilisation from a Field Perspective." Unpublished doctoral dissertation, Education Area, University of Sussex, 1983.

Baskett, H.K.M. "Processes Involved with Developing Autonomous Learning Competencies." In H. B. Long and Associates (eds.), *Self-Directed Learning: Consensus and Conflict.* Norman: Oklahoma Research Center for Continuing Professional and Higher Education, University of Oklahoma, 1991.

Benner, P. *From Novice to Expert: Excellence and Power in Clinical Nursing Practice.* Reading, Mass.: Addison-Wesley, 1984.

Benveniste, G. *Professionalizing the Organization: Reducing Bureaucracy to Enhance Effectiveness.* San Francisco: Jossey-Bass, 1987.

Boud, D., and Griffin, V. (eds.). *Appreciating Adults Learning.* London, England: Kogan Page, 1987.

Burgoyne, J. G., and Hodgson, V. E. "Natural Learning and Managerial Action: A Phenomenological Study in the Field Setting." *Journal of Management Studies,* 1983, *20* (3), 387–399.

Calderhead, J. (ed.). *Teachers' Professional Learning.* London, England: Falmer Press, 1988.

Cervero, R. M., Azzaretto, J. F., and Tallman, D. E. "Renewing and Redirecting Continuing Professional Education." In R. M. Cervero, J. F. Azzaretto, and Associates, *Visions for the Future of Continuing Professional Education.* Athens: Georgia Center for Continuing Education, University of Georgia, 1990.

Curry, L., and Putnam, R. W. "Continuing Medical Education in Maritime Canada: The Methods Physicians Use, Would Prefer, and Find Most Effective." *Canadian Medical Associations Journal,* 1981, *124,* 563–566.

Davies, J., and Easterby-Smith, M. "Learning and Developing from Managerial Work Experiences." *Journal of Management Studies,* 1984, *21* (2), 169–183.

Dechant, K. "Managing Change in the Workplace: Learning Strategies of Managers." Unpublished doctoral dissertation, Teachers College, Columbia University, 1989.

Eraut, M. "Management Knowledge: Its Nature and Its Development." In J. Calderhead (ed.), *Teachers Professional Learning.* London, England: Falmer Press, 1988.

Faure, E. *Learning to Be.* Paris, France: UNESCO, 1972.

Fox, R. D., Maxmanian, P. E., and Putnam, R. W. (eds.). *Changing and Learning in the Lives of Physicians.* New York: Praeger, 1989.

Geertsma, R. H., Parker, R. C., and Whitbourne, S. K. "How Physicians View the Process of Change in Their Practice Behaviour." *Journal of Medical Education,* 1982, *57,* 752–768.

Guskey, T. "Staff Development and the Process of Teacher Change." *Educational Researcher,* 1986, *15* (5), 5–12.

Houle, C. O. *Continuing Learning in the Professions.* San Francisco: Jossey-Bass, 1980.

Hunt, D. E. *Beginning with Ourselves in Theory, Practice, and Human Affairs.* Toronto, Ontario, Canada: Ontario Institute for Studies in Education Press, 1987.

Knox, A. B. "What Difference Does It Make?" In A. B. Knox (ed.), *Assessing the Impact of Continuing Education.* New Directions for Adult and Continuing Education, no. 3. San Francisco: Jossey-Bass, 1979.

Lave, J. *Cognition in Practice.* Cambridge, England: Cambridge University Press, 1988.

McCatty, C. "Patterns of Learning Projects Among Professional Men." *Alberta Journal of Educational Research,* 1975, *20* (1), 116–129.

Marsick, V. J. "How Managers Learn from Experience: A Swedish Experiment." In V. J. Marsick and K. E. Watkins, *Informal and Incidental Learning in the Workplace.* New York: Routledge & Kegan Paul, 1990.

Matthias, M. R. "A Comparative Study of Continuing Competence Among Male Members of Selected Professions." Unpublished doctoral dissertation, Department of Education, University of Toronto, 1991.

Mezirow, J. "A Critical Theory of Adult Learning and Education." *Adult Education,* 1981, *32* (1), 3–24.

Miller, D. B. *Managing Professionals in Research and Development: A Guide for Improving Productivity and Organizational Effectiveness.* San Francisco: Jossey-Bass, 1986.

Nowlen, P. M. "New Expectations, New Roles: A Holistic Approach to Continuing Education for the Professions." In R. M. Cervero, J. F. Azzaretto, and Associates, *Visions for the Future of Continuing Professional Education.* Athens: Georgia Center for Continuing Education, University of Georgia, 1990.

Raelin, J. A. *The Clash of Cultures: Managers and Professionals.* Boston: Harvard Business School Press, 1985.

Rymell, R. G. "How Much Time Do Employed Engineers Spend Learning?" *Engineering Education,* 1981, 72 (2), 172–174.

Schön, D. A. *The Reflective Practitioner: How Professionals Think in Action.* New York: Basic Books, 1983.

Spear, G., and Mocker, D. "The Organizing Circumstance: Environmental Determinants in Self-Directed Learning." *Adult Education Quarterly,* 1984, 35 (1), 1–10.

Sternberg, R. J., and Wagner, R. K. *Practical Intelligence: Nature and Origins of Competence in the Everyday World.* Cambridge, England: Cambridge University Press, 1986.

Tough, A. *Adults' Learning Projects.* Toronto, Ontario, Canada: Ontario Institute for Studies in Education Press, 1971.

Tough, A. "Major Learning Efforts: Recent Research and Future Directions." *Adult Education,* 1978, 28 (4), 250–263.

Zemke, R. "The Honeywell Studies: How Managers Learn to Manage." *Training,* Aug. 1985, pp. 46–51.

H. K. MORRIS BASKETT is professor and program director, Faculty of Continuing Education, University of Calgary, Calgary, Alberta, Canada.

VICTORIA J. MARSICK is associate professor of adult and continuing education at Teachers College, Columbia University in New York City. She currently consults with both the private and public sectors on the design of learning organizations and training approaches.

How do professionals determine what they need to know to perform effectively? Self-assessment is one way to help professionals better understand their learning needs.

Self-Assessment: Helping Professionals Discover What They Do Not Know

Deborah R. Klevans, Wayne D. Smutz,
Susan B. Shuman, Carolyn Bershad

Acquisition of a recognized body of expert knowledge and skills is fundamental to the concept of professionalism. Throughout their careers, however, professionals must continually expand and transform their knowledge and skills to reflect advances in their fields. But how do professionals discover what they do not know and cannot do? One answer is self-assessment. Self-assessment is a systematic approach to the challenge of staying current, an approach that provides educational guidance while leaving individual learners in control of their own professional development.

Foundations of Self-Assessment

The purpose of self-assessment is to help professionals better understand their profession-related learning needs so that they can tailor plans for their professional development. Self-assessment does not refer to self-perceived learning needs but rather to a self-administered testing process that provides confidential, personal information to participants based on external, profession-defined criteria.

Enhancement of the relationship between continuing professional education and performance is important for a number of reasons. First, the growth of knowledge and technology in the professions necessitates continuing professional education for future social and economic development. With this in mind, individuals and organizations who spend considerable time and money to improve performance expect and deserve a substantial return for their investment. Second, for some professionals, continuing education is mandatory. Although the rate of growth in professions requiring continuing education is not nearly as high as it was in the 1970s, the number of professions affected continues to consistently rise (Phillips, 1991). Finally, professionals have a responsibility to the clients whom they serve. By virtue of their specialized expertise and the resultant trust engendered in their clients, professionals are obligated to provide the best service or care possible. Continuing education is one way of developing the capability for providing quality service.

Traditional perspectives tend to interfere with the task of effecting an optimal relationship between education and performance. For example, continuing professional education often is viewed as program planning rather than as a comprehensive educational process. Programming in this sense pertains to the process of communicating information by various means. And yet, effective education also involves identifying what needs to be learned, delivering the content in a way that optimizes learning, and developing strategies to foster the transfer of new learning to practice.

Viewed from the learner's perspective, the programming emphasis in continuing professional education rests on the assumption that professionals are skilled lifelong learners. Continuing educators implicitly assume that professionals can identify their own learning needs, effectively select appropriate learning experiences, determine the most relevant material from the learning experiences chosen, and then transfer the learning to practice. It is unlikely, however, that most professionals acquire the requisite skills to be effective lifelong learners in their preprofessional and professional education programs. With some exceptions, a fostering of self-direction and independence in learning is not characteristic of those levels of education.

Self-assessment represents one technique through which professionals can take responsibility for their professional development. By grounding the process in professional practice, individuals should be in an informed position to select learning activities that have an immediate and direct relationship to that practice. The intent of self-assessment is to empower individuals to more effectively engage in performance-related continuing education.

Elements of a Vision for Self-Assessment

Our vision for a self-assessment process consists of four key elements. First, learning resources, tools that individuals can use to more effectively and efficiently pursue professional development, are needed to provide assistance without usurping the individual's authority in the learning process (Smutz and Queeney, 1990). Second, the individual professional must be the focus of the process. Our goal is to show individuals their unique strengths and weaknesses while maintaining strict confidentiality. Third, the assessment process should be an educational activity in the sense that it exposes professionals to new terms, concepts, and skills and offers them a structured opportunity to reflect on their practice. And, finally, the individualized report of their performance on the self-assessment should motivate participants to engage in continuing education activities. More specifically, we expect that professionals who participate in self-assessment will act on the deficiencies uncovered.

Architecture Example

Since 1987, Pennsylvania State University has worked with the American Institute of Architects (AIA) to develop a self-assessment system for architects and other design professionals. The impetus for the system emerged from an earlier project in which both organizations participated. Sponsored by the W. K. Kellogg Foundation and the university, the 1980–1985 Continuing Professional Education Development Project focused on identifying the learning needs of Pennsylvania professionals through on-site performance assessments using techniques such as client simulations and case studies. Among the many findings of that project, three were particularly noteworthy (Queeney and Smutz, 1990): (1) What professionals want to learn and what they need to learn may not be synonymous, even though both are valid. (2) On-site performance assessment is an extremely expensive tool for identifying learning needs. And (3) professionals are interested in their own personal learning needs, not necessarily the learning needs of groups of professionals.

Following that project, representatives from Penn State and the AIA began to discuss the next steps in helping individual architects better understand their learning needs so that they could more effectively pursue professional development. A collaborative project to develop a self-assessment process for architects was the result. Lessons learned from the previous project made it clear that success would depend in part on making the process relatively inexpensive, easy to use, confidential, and personally relevant.

From the outset, the goal was to develop a series of assessment instruments, known as "audits," that would cover the scope of architecture practice. Based on a previous job analysis conducted by the architecture profession, initial estimates suggested that ten instruments would be necessary. Penn State agreed to develop the assessment instruments, score completed instruments, provide confidential feedback to assessment participants, and design related workshops. The AIA agreed to identify content experts, market the assessment products, and administer the distribution of assessment instruments and the provision of workshops and other educational activities. After completing the first three instruments, the parties agreed to accelerate the development process by creating four new audits in fifteen months. There are now seven instruments available.

Development of Self-Assessment Instruments. All of the individuals involved with the project agreed that the materials developed should reflect high standards and state-of-the-art practices. A development team assigned to produce each self-assessment implemented this vision. Coordinated by continuing professional education specialists from Penn State, the development team also included, at different times, one or more subject matter experts identified by the AIA and an educational psychologist specializing in tests and measurement. At each stage of the assessment development process, an architecture profession team, whose role was to provide oversight and guidance throughout the project, reviewed and critiqued the work completed. This advisory committee consisted of architects representing Penn State's Architecture Department, the state professional association, the national registration board responsible for credentialing architects, and the AIA.

For each self-assessment, the development team began its work by preparing a list of learning objectives related to the assessment topic. These objectives were based on profession-specific role delineations and task descriptions that had been generated during the Kellogg Foundation-Penn State Continuing Professional Education Development Project. A review of relevant professional literature and the content experts' practical knowledge also contributed. After the learning objectives were prepared, they were reviewed by architects on the project advisory committee and often by AIA national office staff members as well. Once approved by all concerned, the learning objectives served as the foundation for the self-assessment instrument and any related continuing education activities.

The audit materials were the result of collaboration among development team members. First, a case study was prepared to add interest and provide a context for linking the items to practice. Next, individual items were written. Assessments ranged in length from twenty-four to thirty-four items. A multiple-choice format was used in order to allow for objective, computer-based scoring and feedback. All members of the development team reviewed each others' work, striving to produce assessment items that were clear, relevant, and interesting to practitioners. Once the items were completed and reviewed, they were ready to be pilot tested.

Pilot Testing. A randomly selected group of four hundred AIA members participated in the pilot test of each self-assessment instrument along with a second group, consisting of first- and fifth-year architecture students. They each were sent one of two draft versions of the self-assessment along with a letter, signed by the chief executive officer of the

AIA, describing the project and soliciting their participation. Return rates averaged over 40 percent, remarkably high considering that the subjects had not volunteered as a test group and each instrument takes an hour or more to complete.

Reliability and validity were determined using data obtained from responses to the assessment and demographic items. Demographic characteristics of the sample were compared with characteristics of the entire AIA membership. Scores were compared between practicing architects and architecture students, and among practitioners with varying amounts of experience, education, and self-rated expertise. Point biserial test item correlations also were computed. Because two versions of the assessment instrument were pilot tested, the better of two parallel items was chosen for the final version of the instrument. Once all changes were completed, the audit was published and made available for purchase.

Administration and Scoring. Current procedures for ordering, completing, scoring, and reporting results of self-assessments meet several goals. First, the process is convenient, straightforward, and flexible. Second, it ensures confidentiality for those participating. Third, feedback is provided in a timely manner. Fourth, accurate records are kept of those ordering and completing self-assessment instruments.

Ordering Assessment Instruments. There are several methods by which architects can obtain self-assessment instruments. The original method is to submit an individual order to the AIA's Professional Development Department. Order forms distributed at professional meetings and articles and advertisements in AIA publications provide the needed information.

Another method by which architects receive audits is through registration for an AIA-sponsored workshop related to one of the assessment topics. Begun as a way of introducing professionals to the self-assessment concept, the inclusion of a self-assessment audit in the price of the workshop is promoted in publicity for live programs. Registrants are sent the audit upon registration and encouraged to complete it and mail it in for scoring several weeks prior to attending the workshop. This procedure serves several purposes. It provides workshop participants with a pretest intended to help them reflect on aspects of the workshop topic. Also, the program facilitator is provided with group data prior to the workshop, in which individual scores are not identified. This enables the instructor to tailor the program to the needs of the group. Finally, the procedure of making audits available to those who otherwise might not order them is a form of educational marketing intended to introduce a somewhat complicated concept and product to a new audience.

A third method of obtaining self-assessment audits is through membership in regional or local professional associations or employment in a firm that orders audits and makes them available to individual architects. Not only do the individuals who participate benefit from completing the audits and receiving feedback, but the firm or professional association also receives information to help plan in-service programs for its members. With individual participants' confidentiality ensured, sponsoring organizations who offer self-assessments in quantity are each entitled to a group report summarizing the audit performance of its members.

Completing the Instrument. By whatever means professionals receive a self-assessment, they have considerable flexibility in completing the instrument. They may choose to do so at work or at home, in one sitting or several. Although no references or supplies are required, respondents are free to use any tools to which they normally would have access. The idea is to make the self-assessment process reflect realistic practice as closely as possible.

Scoring and Recording the Results. Respondents are asked to mail their completed self-assessments to the Continuing Education Office of Program Planning at Penn State for scoring. The Office of Program Planning is responsible for maintaining records of all self-assessment participants in a manner that ensures confidentiality of their performance yet enables group data to be used for record keeping, reporting, and research. The office also is responsible for preparing and sending an individualized feedback report to each respondent.

To meet all of these requirements, the office developed a specialized software program. As each instrument is developed, demographic and assessment items, an answer key, learning objectives, and related learning resources are loaded onto computer files for that assessment. As each completed audit is received, the respondent's name, address, social security number, and responses to demographic and assessment items are input. With a few brief commands, an individualized feedback report is generated and then sent to the respondent. It is equally easy to generate group reports for all or a subgroup of those who have completed a given self-assessment instrument.

Individualized Feedback Report. The feedback report was designed to help recipients determine appropriate professional development goals. Each report is accompanied by a memorandum in which the report's components are previewed, the assessment development process is described, and suggestions are made about how the report can be used for professional development purposes.

The feedback report begins by presenting the respondent's total score. That score is then compared with the average of all others who have completed the audit to date, and the average score of a subgroup of audit respondents whose demographic characteristics are similar in regard to the size of the organization in which they work and years of professional experience.

Next, information about each of the assessment items is provided. Listed first is the learning objective on which the item is based. Then the question is presented, followed by the respondent's answer. If the item was answered incorrectly, the correct answer also is provided. The final section of the feedback report provides an annotated list of learning resources for professional development. Organized by delivery modes, each reference, whether for live programs, print materials, or nonprint materials, is linked to the learning objectives for which the respondent answered items incorrectly.

Lessons from Self-Assessment: Professionals' Reactions

In 1991, the Office of Program Planning undertook a study to systematically examine the extent to which the self-assessment process was fulfilling its intended purpose. The study was designed to investigate three broad issues: professionals' reasons for participating in self-assessment, the effect that their participation had on their pursuit of continuing education, and their evaluation of the overall self-assessment process.

A sample of 592 architects who had used self-assessment instruments was asked to complete a survey about their experience. The questionnaire, developed by Penn State in cooperation with the AIA, consisted of thirty-three questions about the audit process and the respondent's demographic characteristics. It was mailed in August 1991. The response rate was 29 percent ($N = 157$), a reasonable rate of return for a survey of this type.

Reasons for Participation. When asked to indicate one or more reasons for completing a self-assessment, the majority reported they did so because it was a method for fulfilling their professional responsibility to keep up to date (77 percent) and/or because they wanted to learn about areas in which they needed further professional development (75 percent). Forty-one percent participated to expand their expertise on the audit topic. When asked to identify the single most important reason for ordering, the most frequent response was a desire to learn more about areas in which professional development was needed.

Effect of Audit Participation. Survey respondents were also asked questions about the ways and extent to which participation in the process influenced their subsequent professional development. Their responses indicated that completion of the audit had been a learning experience. Sixty-nine percent reported that they had learned about their level of expertise on the audit topic, while 46 percent indicated they were led to think about practice applications, and 33 percent were led to think about their expertise in other practice areas. Fifty-one percent characterized the audit experience as an educational planning activity, and about 33 percent felt that they had gained knowledge about the audit topic.

Approximately 33 percent of the participants reported pursuing additional learning after receiving their feedback report; another 48 percent planned to do so. Pursuit of reading materials listed in the report was the most common learning method chosen (60 percent), followed by discussion of the topic with colleagues (48 percent).

Evaluation of the Self-Assessment Process. A clear majority (69 percent) of survey respondents rated their participation in the self-assessment process as positive. Approximately half noted that feedback data comparing their respective performances on the audit with those of their peers was particularly useful. Eighty-one percent said that they would recommend the process to a colleague, and 66 percent would order an audit on another topic. Taken as a whole, the survey results suggest that architects who have used the self-assessment audits found them educational as well as practical tools for planning their professional development.

Lessons from Self-Assessment: The Developers' Perspective

As is likely in any innovative effort, early experience brought hard-earned lessons. Some were anticipated, others surprising. These issues and attempts at solutions are summarized below.

Lack of Consensus Regarding Professional Knowledge. In architecture, as in other professions, practice is constantly evolving, and legitimate differences of philosophy and perspective exist among highly respected professionals. While these factors affect preparation of entry-level credentialing exams, they are even more of a concern in relation to advanced practice, which often is characterized by ambiguity and the need for idiosyncratic problem solving. This concern, as it applies to development of audits, is partially dealt with by choosing highly respected content experts, using current reference materials, and asking profession leaders to review materials throughout the development process. Also, in the feedback material sent to respondents, practitioners are encouraged to recognize that consensus may not exist and to reflect on alternative perspectives, including those with which they may disagree.

Legal Implications for Individuals and Organizations. An unanticipated issue arose when legal counsel for the AIA raised concerns about whether the self-assessment instruments might be seen to reflect a standard of care, that is, the "law's underlying minimum expectation for the performance of professionals" (Abramowitz, 1988, p. 3). If that were the case, then a report of an architect's performance on a self-assessment instrument could be subpoenaed should he or she be sued for malpractice. Opposing legal counsel might then question the competence of an architect who did not score well on the assessment or ask what follow-up actions were taken to address any limitations or learning needs identified.

To allay these possibilities, however remote, several steps were taken.

First, the learning objectives and assessment items were written with language that does not imply a standard of care. In addition, the memorandum accompanying the feedback report states that "the self-assessment audit process is not intended to establish a universal standard of care, but rather to assist you in identifying your professional development needs on this component of architectural practice." Finally, all materials were reviewed and approved by AIA legal counsel prior to publication.

Individuals' Desire to Receive Answers to the Assessment Items. Development of a feedback report that is economical to produce, encourages recipients to focus on their professional development needs in relation to learning objectives, and is informative but not too complex or lengthy involved some difficult choices. An initial decision was to produce a report that did not include answers to assessment items. It was reasoned that inclusion of all items and answers not only would make the report too long but also would enable an architect who completed the process to share both items and answers with colleagues who otherwise might order the assessment for themselves. Although recipients were generally pleased with the feedback reports, many were disappointed and frustrated that the reports did not include answers to each item. After consistent requests for answers, the feedback report was modified to include answers.

Conclusion

Self-assessment represents our attempt to increase the effectiveness of continuing professional education by helping individuals better understand their learning needs. Our effort to bring the self-assessment system to fruition for architects is truly a developmental process. While there are many ways in which the process might be improved, the study indicates that the key aspects of our vision for self-assessment are being realized. Individuals are using the self-assessment process as a learning resource to help them better understand their profession-based learning needs and they are enjoying the experience. Self-assessment is perceived as an educational activity in and of itself. Participants indicate that they gain new knowledge about matters with which they are unfamiliar, and that the process leads them to reflect on their own practice. Finally, self-assessment stimulates most participants to plan for and engage in both informal and formal continuing education activities.

Development of the self-assessment system for architects was Penn State's first effort to use this approach, but it is only one such effort. Professional associations for physicians have been developing self-assessment projects for some time (Davidoff, 1989). Several other professions are exploring the possibility of developing similar self-assessment systems.

Recently, Penn State's Continuing Education Office of Program Planning began development of a self-assessment system for dietitians under the sponsorship of the American Dietetic Association Commission on Dietetic Registration. Although dietitians, unlike architects, must meet mandatory continuing education requirements, the system is similar in many ways to the architecture self-assessment. As a second-generation system, however, it has made substantial advances over its predecessor. The assessment instruments are more complex and more realistic.

It has become apparent that self-assessment has value for individuals across professions, regardless of whether continuing education is mandatory. Although the costs of self-assessment systems vary depending on their level of sophistication, the task of developing quality materials, an efficient administrative structure, and an effective marketing strategy can be costly and labor-intensive. For that reason, some continuing educators may need to consider other means of attaining the ultimate goal of the self-assessment process, to help individuals closely examine and reflect on their practice in order to better understand their learning needs. Alternative approaches include use of the critical incident technique or chart audits to uncover problem areas in practice and peer learning projects that enable professionals to obtain systematic feedback from colleagues. These approaches and others can provide professionals with insight and information about their professional development needs. The important point is that professionals need assistance if they are to benefit optimally from continuing professional education. Self-assessment is proving to be one important way to provide that assistance.

References

Abramowitz, A. "The Legal Environment." In D. Haviland (ed.), *The Architect's Handbook of Professional Practice*. Washington, D.C.: AIA Press, 1987.

Davidoff, F. "The American College of Physicians and the Medical Knowledge Self-Assessment Program Paradigm." *Journal of Continuing Education in the Health Professions*, 1989, 9, 233–238.

Phillips, L. *Newsletter*. Athens, Ga.: Louis Phillips and Associates, 1991.

Queeney, D. S., and Smutz, W. D. "Enhancing the Performance of Professionals: The Practice-Audit Model." In S. L. Willis, S. S. Dubin, and Associates, *Maintaining Professional Competence: Approaches to Career Enhancement, Vitality, and Success Throughout a Work Life*. San Francisco: Jossey-Bass, 1990.

Smutz, W. D., and Queeney, D. S. "Professionals as Learners: A Strategy for Maximizing Professional Growth." In R. M. Cervero, J. F. Azzaretto, and Associates, *Visions for the Future of Continuing Professional Education*. Athens: Georgia Center for Continuing Education, University of Georgia, 1990.

DEBORAH R. KLEVANS, *research and planning associate;* WAYNE D. SMUTZ, *acting director; and* CAROLYN BERSHAD, *research project associate, are all affiliated with the Continuing Education Office of Program Planning, Pennsylvania State University, University Park.*

SUSAN B. SHUMAN *is a research and planning analyst for the Continuing Education Office of Market Research, Pennsylvania State University.*

Provision of learning opportunities at the practice site that are practitioner-directed and experience-based and are organized around practice problems and context yields special benefits. The professional need not leave the work environment, and consequently, travel costs are reduced, potential income and productivity are enhanced, and what is learned is more likely to be applied immediately.

Educational Responses to Practice-Based Learning: Recent Innovations in Medicine

Penny A. Jennett, Thomas G. Pearson

Professional practice is continually challenged by the impact of changing expectations, shifting standards of care, information and technological advancements, and the need for new skills. Professionals, therefore, face a complex and uncertain environment that demands ongoing learning and change. In response to this reality, a consolidation of literature has recently developed that offers new ideas about how professionals can optimally acquire professional competence, keep current, and learn (Knowles, 1990; Fox, Maxmanian, and Putnam, 1989; Nowlen, 1988; Schön, 1983; Cervero, 1990).

Professionals seek learning that is practitioner-directed, experience-based, and organized around practice problems and context (Knowles, 1990; Houle, 1980). Learning involves both abstract (formal, general, passive) and practical (practice-based, specific, active) knowledge; the reflective act of practice is an essential ingredient (Cervero, 1990; Schön, 1983). Learning that is practice-linked; incorporates professional, personal, social, and environmental factors; and facilitates networking with both experts and peers has been found to enhance both performance change and outcome (Fox, Maxmanian, and Putnam, 1989; Nowlen, 1988).

In the past, especially in medicine, there has been a strong tradition of formalized, didactic undergraduate education, centered in the lecture hall with a highly structured, less than flexible curriculum. One residual effect of this introduction to rigidly structured medical education is that many practitioners who graduate from medical school bring the same approaches and assumptions to their lifelong learning. In recent years, continuing professional education (CPE) has been increasingly directed by individual needs and day-to-day challenges and thus has provided more flexible options for the learner to partake in individualized and self-directed learning activities. There has been a move away from traditional lockstep approaches that focus on the educational needs of the group to those that respond to the needs of the individual practitioner.

Provision of educational opportunities at the practice site (whether traditional, self-directed, and/or technology-oriented) offers definite economic incentives to health care professionals. Whether one considers physicians in their practice or allied health workers based at a patient care institution, the benefits are considerable to both the individual and the institution if the learner has the option of engaging in productive learning activities without leaving the work environment. Not only are costs reduced by removing the need for travel, but potential income and productivity are enhanced because the individuals are not removed for days at a time from their practice or locales. Furthermore, CPE conducted at the workplace can be highly specific for that learning audience and can center around cases and problems common to that particular institution and its patient mix.

The same technological advancements that have greatly enhanced the quality of medical care are also being applied to the learning methodologies available in CPE for the health professions and are revolutionizing the way that health care personnel approach learning. Technological media such as audiotapes, videotapes, videodisks, slides, print materials, and computer-assisted learning tools are now readily available to professionals for individual study and for data retrieval, organization, and storage. Interactive and on-line computer software packages permit individualized problem solving, clinical decision assessment, information access, and data storage. In addition, audio and video teleconferencing facilitates networking among peers, experts, multiprofessionals, and multisites. Communication packages, such as electronic mail and bulletin boards, offer ready access to peers and experts and provide information at convenient times and places (Manning, 1983; Conrath and others, 1977; Dunn and others, 1977; Jennett and others, 1990a, 1990b; Juckett and Spratt, 1987).

This chapter documents concrete, practical, and innovative applications of CPE by incorporating both current understandings of professional learning and recent technological advances in continuing education. Although the applications discussed here are specific to the profession of medicine, they are relevant to many professional fields.

Recent Innovations

In the 1970s, continuing professional educators applied adult learning and behavioral change principles to innovative CPE activities. Stein (1981) reports on eight such projects that were unique in their approaches to CPE but uniform in their attention to educational principles. Although the programs varied with respect to the clinical condition addressed and to learning objectives (knowledge, skills, and/or attitudes) and differed in educational format, each program had identified learning needs for a specific audience, had clearly stated goals and objectives, emphasized patient problems from the work setting, adopted relevant learning methods for the stated objectives, and systematically evaluated the educational effects. Participatory educational methods were used. In each program, learners recognized their need for improved performance and participated in a needs assessment, in the planning of the educational program, and in the evaluation. Learning and change in physician performance were reported for each of these projects for at least six months. Peer consensus, review, and feedback were central ingredients to a number of the successful programs.

Peer-Based Learning. The conjoined effort of presenting clinical cases, discussing relevant literature, and encouraging feedback from peers and experts is common in hospital settings as a mode of education and as an instrument for quality care. Community hospitals have long recognized the value of providing CPE opportunities for the members of the health care team. Weekly or monthly lectures on aspects of health care, as well as staff development, have been actively supported by many hospitals. Indeed, the Joint Commission for the Accreditation of Healthcare Organizations in the United States and the Canadian Council on Health Facilities Accreditation in Canada have included among their criteria the need for hospitals to provide health care CPE. Traditionally, CPE in hospitals has had the benefit of a strong case discussion, problem-oriented design that can be multidisciplinary in approach.

More recently, because of the current understanding of practice work environments, learning and change, and learning principles, such innovative approaches have been applied to office clinical cases. Premi (1988) describes an innovative problem-based, small group learning activity for practitioners, building on the model of hospital rounds. In this study, physicians brought clinical problems from their individual practices for presentation and discussion twice per month for two-hour sessions. This educational program considered the unique context of the practitioners' personal practices. Feedback from peers, experts, and the literature enhanced the learning process.

The chart audit, a careful review of information within a patient's health record using predefined criteria, is also an innovative tool used for many hospital and office quality-assurance activities. Several approaches to the use of the chart audit have been recorded (Gerbert, Countiss, and Gullion, 1983; Gullion, Adamson, and Watts, 1983; and Jennett and others, 1988). It requires peer and expert consensus on criteria and standards and provides an information baseline by which performance levels can be measured at specific times. Practitioners can identify what their learning needs are and can measure their individual performance against those of peers in a nonthreatening, confidential manner. Jennett and others (1988) found that thirty-one family physicians in office practice could learn and adopt new behaviors in cardiovascular and cancer medicine by engaging in an innovative educational program that consisted of face-to-face and teleconference dialogues with consultants, along with the study of group performance behavior and the sharing of newsletter information. Practice issues identified for learning were discussed by family practitioners, peers, and consultant experts at designated times and through the use of newsletters. Physicians could carry out reading related to the practice issues at their convenience. A similar approach using hospital-based chart audits in small working community hospitals was successful in engaging practitioners and in eliciting positive change (Laxdal, Jennett, Wilson, and Salisbury, 1978). With the recent computerization of medical charts and the capability of storing information in local data banks, ongoing, continuous quality care self-audits conducted by individual sites and physicians are highly practical as an approach to CPE at the work site.

The value of networks among academic centers, experts, educational influentials, and practitioners has been demonstrated through a number of innovative CPE programs. Using the three separate clinical conditions of osteoarthritis, rheumatoid arthritis, and pulmonary disease, Stross and Bole (1980, 1985) and Stross and others (1983) demonstrated that lines of communication could be established within the physician network that could change both hospital and outpatient care in the desired direction. Medical audits of both inpatient and outpatient charts were conducted, and education based on identified target needs was provided to educationally influential physicians, who were consulted frequently by peers. The innovative educational programs were inexpensive, patient-oriented, problem-specific, community-focused, and responsive to the teachable moment. The selected practitioners, who were well respected professionally and personally and thereby influential, acted as information sources for the community. Through various avenues, they affected the practice behaviors of their peers at their local sites.

This type of educational strategy uses identified learning needs of local sites to focus and motivate participants. This approach is the foundation of another innovative CPE focus, practice-based or patient-based education.

Practice-Based Education. The use of practice-based problems for CPE has been repeatedly shown to be one of the most successful techniques for attracting and involving health care professionals in learning activities. The posing of practical problems that have relevance to daily clinical experience normally stimulates more interest in learners than do educational programs that deal with highly abstract, esoteric medical topics or concerns. Premi's (1988) study, described earlier, illustrates this concept. The University of Wisconsin demonstrated early on the merits of working with individual physician practice profiles (Siverston, Meyer, Hansen, and Schoenberger, 1973). Furthermore, Manning (1983, p. 1042) stated that "the next step in CME [continuing medical education] is for hospitals, societies, and medical schools to perfect methods of self-study of practice and practice-limited CME."

As an example, Manning and others (1986) describe an innovative educational approach based on practice-linked information other than direct chart audits. Duplicate prescription pads were used. Prescriptions relating to the ten most commonly prescribed drugs for each of the forty-one participating internists and family physicians were reviewed and analyzed, and appropriate education was targeted to individual practitioners' needs.

Educational mechanisms that respond to day-to-day questions arising in the workplace are one of the most effective approaches to meeting physicians' CPE needs. Covell, Uman, and Manning (1985) studied the information needs of forty-seven internists during a half-day office practice and found that physicians turned to human sources to respond to practice questions 53 percent of the time; patient questions were addressed by the literature approximately 25 percent of the time. Jennett and others (1990a, 1990b) also provided a special CPE program for family practitioners in response to practice questions and issues.

Individual Learning Contracts. A professional's dedication to learning is also known to affect outcome (Manning and others, 1987; Stross and Bole, 1985). Learning contracts typically involve a one- to three-year time commitment during which the learner agrees to participate in such multifaceted programs of learning as attending formal courses, working under the supervision of a mentor in a particular aspect of the discipline, reading selected journals, and/or conducting research. Individual components in the contract integrate discrete educational experiences into an overall plan. The components of this plan specify a long-term learner-designed purpose. Typically, these contracts are evaluated and monitored by a review body of peers such as a hospital education committee or department faculty. The Colorado Personalized Education for Physicians Program, based in Denver, is one example of this approach. To date, thirty-one physicians have participated in the program, with two having now officially graduated (Bunnell, Kahn, Kasunic, Radcliff, 1991).

In several studies, physician-learning contracts have been found to be creative, effective educational opportunities. In an educational program addressing arrhythmia, Crandall (1990) found five experienced practitioners (four family physicians and one internist) who made commitments to make nine changes specific to factual knowledge, clinical judgment, attitudes, and professional and personal lives. Sixty-seven percent of the changes were carried out. Similarly, Manning and colleagues (1986, 1987) reported that learning plans and contracts facilitate professional education. Forty-five specialists completed fifty-five learning projects regarding physician knowledge, clinical skills, and education of others, and forty-seven internists and family physicians changed their habits of prescribing. The authors concluded that similar self-directed learning activities could be used for CPE and specialist board recertification requirements.

Self-Assessment. Many practitioners recognize the value of a combination of both traditional and innovative CME events but prefer self-learning and self-assessment activities that they can carry out in their workplaces, at chosen times and in an inexpensive fashion (Pearson, 1988; Kilani, 1991). CME activities and reward systems are accommodating these preferences. Sophisticated and formalized assessment programs such as the American College of Physicians Self-Assessment Program have achieved considerable popularity among physician learners as a means for determining personal learning needs. The American Board of Family Practice and the College of Family Physicians of Canada incorporated self-assessment strategies into their recertification and maintenance of certification processes in the 1970s. Five years ago, the American College of Obstetricians and Gynecologists developed a series of computer-based patient management problems titled "ACOG Interactions— Programs in Clinical Decision Making." This very popular program challenges learners with questions related to the diagnosis and management of a particular patient. In addition, it offers review loops and has an underlying management decision tree built into the software, as well as relevant literature references and abstracts.

Recently, the Royal College of Physicians and Surgeons of Canada incorporated a planned CME program titled "The Maintenance of Competence (MOCOMP)." In this project, throughout the educational process, practicing specialists participate on planning committees, identify learning needs that are ideally derived from practice, receive feedback, and interact with others. The number of credits assigned for an educational program is related to the application of adult learning principles within it. Many medical specialty societies and the American Medical Association recently elevated the value of Category 2 (informal) learning, which recognizes and supports basic principles regarding the nature of adult learning. Informal experience-based learning can then be effectively applied in such areas as self-directed learning, practice-linked education, and current educational technology. Indeed, technology has given rise to many new and exciting approaches to CPE.

Technology. The precepts of adult learning theory support the use of technology as innovative methods in CPE (Knowles, 1990; Houle, 1980). Likewise, the availability of technological hardware and software in the practice site and at home is increasing continually. Case histories, simulations, and patient management problems conducted through such delivery systems as computer, interactive videodisk, videotape, and teleconferencing can all build on the learner's previous clinical experience and clinical reasoning skills. The cumulative clinical background of the learner is incorporated in "solving" simulated case problems presented in this manner (Siegel and Parrino, 1988). Telephone lines, fax communications, and computerized communication networks provide rapid exchanges and information and feedback.

Lindsay and others (1987) describe the telemedicine program for health professionals in Ontario, an interactive audio system that links individual site telephone lines to a centrally located switchboard bridge. The advancement of this technology provides the opportunity for inexpensive CPE to multisites and multiprofessionals. Such audio teleconferencing programs are now routinely offered by many academic CPE centers in provinces across Canada and in the United States. Slides and printed material can be precirculated to supplement the audio.

Jennett and others (1990b) designed a special CPE program that provides reading materials for practice issues. Telephone lines, fax communications, and computer technology were all incorporated to respond to practice needs in a timely and efficient manner. Forty-seven primary care physicians phoned in 240 day-to-day practice questions of a nonemergency nature for over a ten-month period. Reading materials on identified practice issues were retrieved using off-line or on-line computer software search packages. Retrieved information was validated by relevant consultants and faxed to the requesting sites. In addition, a newsletter network exchange, focusing on common questions, was established between local practices and the academic university CME center. The resulting question data base represents real practice needs and is being used not only for the education of individual practitioners but also for educational benefits related to the selected practice sites. Short two-hour sessions on literature searches were offered to enhance the skills of local physicians who elected to use local hardware and software computer capabilities to search the literature directly as opposed to using the centralized service.

Learner readiness, cost considerations, and hardware obsolescence are important considerations when using technology for educational purposes. Even when computers are optimal for learning activities, there exist the potential problems of computer illiteracy and "cyberphobia" (Lloyd, 1984). For these reasons, there is a need to train learners on technology use before educational activities can or should be conducted. Included with skills training, there is also a need to encourage attitudinal change among those whose resistance to technology is based on unnecessary scepticism or lack of information (Allan and Walraven, 1987).

Implications for CME Practitioners, Planners, and Organizations

How can continuing educators help professionals with self-directed learning activities at the practice site? Those involved have a number of interventions and approaches at their disposal.

CME Planners and Organizations. First, they can help practitioners make the transition from dependent learners to self-directed learners by involving them in the identification of learning needs and the selection of methods, resources, and evaluation approaches (Knowles, 1990). They can provide guidance on how to phrase questions (Covell, Uman, and Manning, 1985), prepare validated reviews and expert networks (Williamson and others, 1989), assist in techniques that permit them to examine their own performance (Knowles, 1990), help them to identify learning needs, and assist them in clarifying what they want to learn (Knowles, 1990; Richards, 1984).

CPE models, based on contemporary views of adult learning, are also now available for educational planners. Knowles (1990) and Root-Bernstein (1987) suggest a learning model that considers society and the health care system, where supportive and collaborative relationships are established between faculty and learners and where faculty are facilitators rather than instructors. Fox, Maxmanian, and Putnam (1989) indicate continuing educators can assist learners in recognizing where they are, where they wish to go, and what they need to learn. CPE educators must consider forces for change and types of learning. Nowlen (1988) suggests that CPE organizations must appreciate the context in which their learners practice and understand how innovation and change occur within that context. Cervero (1990) describes a learning model based on practice where uncertainty, judgment, and intuition operate in a specific context. Such learning requires both formal and practical knowledge.

Practitioners. Workplace-centered learning and appropriate innovative technology have practical implications for the professional. Ongoing self-directed learning activities from the practice environment provide the practitioner with the mechanism to respond to changes within the profession and society in general. This type of learning, because of its practical nature, can enhance practice behavior and change. It is an efficient, low-cost approach to keeping up to date as each practitioner can approach learning at a time, pace, and location appropriate to individual needs. In addition, it fosters integration and confirmation of experience in practice, that is, makes experience the basis of learning.

To accommodate to this type of learning, practitioners must cultivate and foster skills that enable them to take major responsibility for ongoing learning. They must take the initiative in identifying, assessing, and setting the priorities for learning specific to their needs. They must grow to naturally define goals, seek and organize learning activities, and evaluate outcomes (Knox, 1973; Tough, 1971). Practitioners must be at ease with both traditional and self-directed innovative approaches to learning and must cultivate lifelong learning skills and habits that permit them to incorporate into daily practice the reflective art of practice, the goal of continuous improvement, and the skills for information management (Schön, 1983, 1987; Berwick, 1989; Williamson and others, 1989).

In the planning of these educational activities, the selection of an appropriate methodology or technique is dependent on a number of variables. These include the specified learning objectives, individual learning style of participants, number of learners involved in the experience, budgetary limitations, complexity of the content, and level of learning to be achieved. All of these variables must be considered and evaluated before a particular method or approach is selected. Attention to available adult education models and approaches, as well as a study of documented effective applications, will facilitate appropriate integration and progress.

Cost considerations are also important. Computers, satellite linkups, and laser disks all require substantial funding, and in an era of increasing concern for cost containment it can be difficult to justify such expenditures. The cost factor of educational technology is heightened by the problem of hardware obsolescence. The hardware may be out of date shortly after the decision to purchase it or the arrival of the system. These challenges are decreasing in magnitude but still are important issues for CPE planners and practitioners.

Conclusion

Recent insight into professional learning, preferred methods of professional learning, and technical advances in educational media support and reinforce both practice-based learning and innovative approaches to this learning. These directions build on the learning precepts of adult education (Knowles, 1970, 1990; Houle, 1980) and support the philosophy of continuous improvement outlined by Berwick (1989). They are in keeping with the ultimate desire of both professionals and professional bodies to find optimal ways of keeping professionally up to date on an ongoing basis. Learner responsibilities and skills required to pursue this type of learning in an optimal fashion require facilitation and support.

One of the greatest benefits that practice-based CPE can offer learners is convenience. Participants can access and actively complete learning activities at their own paces. The increased prevalence of technology software and hardware at practice sites and in health care professionals' homes has enhanced the convenience factor for this type of learning.

In looking toward the future of education for the health professions, it is apparent that learning opportunities in the work setting will only expand in usefulness and availability. As CPE continues to become more self-directed and self-diagnostic, patient care institutions and physicians' offices will become ideal locations for lifelong learning to take place. The price of technological hardware and software for education will continue to decrease, thus making its purchase more affordable. Likewise, highly focused CPE activities such as personal learning plans or learning contracts will heighten the sense of "ownership" and personal responsibility of health professionals in the design and implementation of their learning activities.

References

Allan, D. M., and Walraven, G. "Issues in the Adoption of New Educational Technology." *Computer Methods Programs Biomed,* 1987, *25* (2), 103–109.

Berwick, D. M. "Continuous Improvement as an Ideal in Health Care." *New England Journal of Medicine,* Jan. 5, 1989, pp. 53–57.

Bunnell, K. P., Kahn, K. A., Kasunic, L. B., and Radcliff, S. "Development of a Model for Personalized Continuing Medical Education." *Journal of Continuing Education in the Health Professions,* 1991, *11* (1), 19–27.

Cervero, R. M. "The Importance of Practical Knowledge and Implications for Continuing Education." *Journal of Continuing Education in the Health Professions,* 1990, *10* (1), 85–94.

Conrath, D., and others. "A Clinical Evaluation of Four Alternative Telemedicine Systems." *Behavioral Science,* 1977, *22,* 12–21.

Covell, D. G., Uman, G. C., and Manning, P. R. "Information Needs in Office Practice: Are They Being Met?" *Annals of Internal Medicine,* 1985, *103,* 596–599.

Crandall, S.J.S. "The Role of Continuing Medical Education in Changing and Learning." *Journal of Continuing Education in the Health Professions,* 1990, *10* (4), 339–348.

Dunn, E. V., and others. "An Evaluation of Four Telemedicine Systems for Primary Care." *Health Services Research,* 1977, *12,* 19–29.

Fox, R. D., Maxmanian, P. E., and Putnam, R. W. (eds.). *Changing and Learning in the Lives of Physicians.* New York: Praeger, 1989.

Gerbert, B., Countiss, R. B., and Gullion, D. S. "Agreement Among Four Physician Performance Assessment Methods: In Search of a 'Gold Standard.'" In *Continuing Medical Education: Measurement Issues on Trial.* Proceedings of the 22nd Annual Conference. Washington, D.C.: Association of American Medical Colleges, 1983.

Gullion, D. S., Adamson, T. E., and Watts, M.S.M. "The Effect of an Individualized Practice-Based CME Program on Physician Performance and Patient Outcome." *Western Journal of Medicine,* 1983, *138,* 582–588.

Houle, C. O. *Continuing Learning in the Professions.* San Francisco: Jossey-Bass, 1980.

Jennett, P. A., and others. "The Effects of C.M.E. upon Family Physician Performance in Office Practice: A Randomized Controlled Study." *Medical Education,* 1988, *22,* 139–145.

Jennett, P. A., and others. "A Medical Information Networking System Between Practitioners and Academia: Its Role in the Maintenance of Competence." *Journal of Continuing Education in the Health Professions,* 1990a, *10* (3), 237–243.

Jennett, P. A., and others. "Providing Relevant Information to Rural Practitioners: A Study of a Medical Information System." *Teaching and Learning in Medicine,* 1990b, 2 (4), 200–204.

Jennett, P. A., and others. "Preparing Doctors for Tomorrow. Information Management as a Theme in Undergraduate Medical Education." *Medical Education,* 1991, 25, 135–139.

Juckett, M., and Spratt, J. S. "What Is the Value of the Computer for the Physician?" *Journal of Surgical Oncology,* 1987, 34 (1), 1–5.

Kilani, E. (ed.). *AMA Continuing Medical Education Fact Sheet.* Chicago: American Medical Association, 1991.

Knowles, M. S. *The Modern Practice of Adult Education.* New York: Association Press, 1970.

Knowles, M. S. *The Adult Learner: A Neglected Species.* Houston, Tex.: Gulf, 1990.

Knox, A. B. "Lifelong Self-Directed Education." In *Fostering the Growing Need to Learn.* Monograph and Annotated Bibliography on Continuing Education and Health Manpower. Rockville, Md.: Health Resources Administration, Public Health Service, U.S. Department of Health, Education, and Welfare, 1973.

Laxdal, O. E., Jennett, P. A., Wilson, T. W., and Salisbury, G. M. "Improving Physician Performance by Continuing Medical Education." *Canadian Medical Association Journal,* 1978, 118, 1051–1058.

Lindsay, E. A., and others. "Continuing Education Through Telemedicine for Ontario." *Canadian Medical Association Journal,* 1987, 137, 503–506.

Lloyd, J. S. (ed.). *Computer Applications to the Evaluation of Physician Competence.* Chicago: American Board of Medical Specialties, 1984.

Manning, P. R. "Continuing Medical Education: The Next Step." *Journal of the American Medical Association,* 1983, 249 (8), 1042–1045.

Manning, P. R., and others. "Changing Prescribing Practices Through Individual Continuing Education." *Journal of the American Medical Association,* 1986, 256 (2), 230–232.

Manning, P. R., and others. "A Method of Self-Directed Learning in Continuing Medical Education with Implications for Recertification." *Annals of Internal Medicine,* 1987, 107, 909–913.

Nowlen, P. M. *A New Approach to Continuing Education for Business and the Professions.* New York: Macmillan, 1988.

Pearson, T. G. "American Academy of Dermatology Membership Survey on Self-Assessment and Other CME Activities." Paper presented at the Congress on Continuing Medical Education, Los Angeles, April 27–May 1, 1988.

Premi, J. N. "Problem-Based, Self-Directed Continuing Medical Education in a Group of Practicing Family Physicians." *Journal of Medical Education,* 1988, 63, 484–486.

Richards, R. K. "Physician Learning and Individualized CME." *MOBIUS,* 1984, 4 (2), 165–170.

Root-Bernstein, R. S. "Tools of Thought: Designing an Integrated Curriculum for Lifelong Learners." *Roeper Review,* 1987, 10 (1), 17–21.

Schön, D. A. *The Reflective Practitioner: How Professionals Think in Action.* New York: Basic Books, 1983.

Schön, D. A. *Educating the Reflective Practitioner: Toward a New Design for Teaching and Learning in the Professions.* San Francisco: Jossey-Bass, 1987.

Siegel, J. D., and Parrino, T. A. "Computerized Diagnosis: Implications for Clinical Education." *Medical Education,* 1988, 22 (1), 47–54.

Siverston, S. E., Meyer, T. C., Hansen, R., and Schoenberger, A. "Individual Physician Practice Profile: Continuing Education Related to Medical Practice." *Journal of Medical Education,* 1973, 48, 1006–1012.

Stein, L. S. "The Effectiveness of Continuing Medical Education: Eight Research Reports." *Journal of Medical Education,* 1981, 56, 103–110.

Stross, J. K., and Bole, G. G. "Evaluation of a Continuing Education Program in Rheumatoid Arthritis." *Arthritis and Rheumatism,* 1980, 23 (7), 846–849.

Stross, J. K., and Bole, G. G. "Evaluation of an Educational Program for Primary Care Practitioners, on the Management of Osteoarthritis." *Arthritis and Rheumatism,* 1985, 28 (1), 108–111.

Stross, J. K., and others. "Continuing Education in Pulmonary Disease for Primary Care Physicians." *American Review of Respiratory Diseases,* 1983, *127,* 739–746.

Tough, A. *Adults' Learning Projects.* Toronto, Ontario, Canada: Ontario Institute for Studies in Education Press, 1971.

Williamson, D. W., and others. "Health Science Information Management and the Continuing Education of Physicians—A Survey of U.S. Primary Care Practitioners and Their Opinion Leaders." *Annals of Internal Medicine,* 1989, *110,* 151–160.

PENNY A. JENNETT *is associate professor and director, Office of Medical Education, Faculty of Medicine, University of Calgary, Calgary, Alberta, Canada.*

THOMAS G. PEARSON *is director of education at the American Academy of Dermatology, Schaumburg, Illinois.*

According to a practitioner, "The hallmark of the professional is being able to understand and deal proficiently with ill-defined, risky, and complex problems, not just the less challenging ones." Cognitive apprenticeship is an instructional tool particularly well suited to teaching practitioners to understand and deal proficiently with difficult problems. It can complement currently used forms of continuing professional education.

Cognitive Apprenticeship: Implications for Continuing Professional Education

James A. Farmer, Jr., Annette Buckmaster, Barbara LeGrand

One of the authors of this chapter, James A. Farmer, Jr., interviewed 450 practitioners in five professions about the forms of instruction that they found most meaningful and helpful in learning to understand and deal satisfactorily with ill-defined, complex, and risky situations (Johnson and Farmer, 1989; Farmer, Schafer, and Lippert, 1983; Farmer, 1983). Interviewees stated that what helps most is being taught by someone who models how to understand and deal with such situations and who then guides the learners' attempts to do the real thing. This type of instruction was subsequently identified as a form of cognitive apprenticeship. The use of cognitive apprenticeship in continuing professional education is the focus of this chapter.

Our literature review revealed that although cognitive apprenticeship (Brown, Collins, and Duguid, 1989; Collins, Brown, and Newman, 1989) has been used successfully to help children, youth, and college-age students learn reading, writing, and mathematics, there were no descriptions of cognitive apprenticeship developed specifically for use with professionals. We have studied forms of cognitive apprenticeship used in several professions, including aviation, engineering, orthopedic surgery, veterinary medicine, educational administration, and program management (Prestine and LeGrand, 1991; Johnson and Farmer, 1989; Farmer, Lippert, and Schafer, 1991; Buckmaster, Farmer, and LeGrand, 1990).

NEW DIRECTIONS FOR ADULT AND CONTINUING EDUCATION, no. 55, Fall 1992 © Jossey-Bass Publishers

Along with others, we have used cognitive apprenticeship in a variety of continuing professional education settings and have found that it teaches individuals how to think and act satisfactorily in practice. It transmits useful, reliable knowledge, based on the consensual agreement of practitioners, about how to deal with situations, particularly those that are ill-defined, complex, and risky. It teaches "knowledge-in-action" that is "situated" (Brown, Collins, and Duguid, 1989) in the profession.

Using Cognitive Apprenticeship with Professionals

Cognitive apprenticeship starts with deliberate instruction by someone who acts as a model; it then proceeds to model-guided trials by practitioners who progressively assume more responsibility for their learning. Learners bring their full biographies (Jarvis, 1987; Farmer, Buckmaster, and LeGrand, 1989) to cognitive apprenticeship. Biographical information can be used to match learners with the cognitive apprenticeship experiences most likely to be beneficial. A minimum of prerequisite or "enriching" information is provided prior to the cognitive apprenticeship experience in accordance with the cognitivist, holistic, or top-down approach to instruction (West, Farmer, and Wolff, 1991).

Cognitive apprenticeship adapted for use in continuing professional education consists of the following five sequential phases. Words in italic are used similarly to their usage in descriptions of other forms of cognitive apprenticeship.

Phase 1. At the heart of cognitive apprenticeship is *modeling* a professional activity that the learner wants to be able to perform satisfactorily in the real world. This modeling combines behavioral modeling (Perry and Furukawa, 1980) and cognitive modeling (Meichenbaum, 1977; Gist, 1989). Modeling is conducted by an individual (or individuals) who is able to perform the activity acceptably well. The key here is that learners observe the model perform the entire activity, not merely subskills. This enables learners to develop a mental model, a schema, of what doing the real thing looks like.

During the behavioral modeling, cognitive modeling occurs as the model states aloud (*articulates*) the essence of his or her thinking. This may include the "tricks of the trade" (*domain-specific heuristics*) that help one do the real thing.

Phase 2. After observing the modeling, learners approximate doing the real thing while articulating the essence of their thoughts. The articulation includes stating prior to action what they plan to do and why. Learners are encouraged to *reflect* on the differences between their performance and the model's performance in order to develop self-monitoring and self-correction skills. Reflection is facilitated by discussion, alternation of model and learner activities, and learner problem solving under guidance. Learners' efforts to do the real thing are *scaffolded* to minimize risks. Scaffolding consists of supports, such as physical aids, or of having the model carry out part of the task, which helps the learners approximate doing the real thing as much as possible. The model *coaches* the learners, supplying feedback about their performance and suggesting improvements. Remediation is provided as necessary, based on the difficulties learners evince in the scaffolded performance.

Phase 3. Learners, individually or in groups, continue to approximate doing the real thing. Coaching and scaffolding decrease (the *fading* process) as learners' ability to do the real thing increases.

Phase 4. This *internalizing* phase starts when learners are able to approximate doing the real thing satisfactorily (sometimes only after a series of successive approximations). In this phase, they learn to do the real thing on their own (self-directed learning) and in their own ways within specified limits acceptable to the profession and society. Assistance is provided only on request.

Phase 5. The model and the learners discuss the *generalizability* of what has been learned. This discussion can serve as an advance organizer (West, Farmer, and Wolff, 1991), relating what has been learned in the cognitive apprenticeship experience to the task of learning subsequently how to understand and deal satisfactorily with other types of situations. "Situation-specific learning by itself is very limiting" (Resnick, 1987, p. 15). This phase helps ensure that learning will generalize appropriately.

Example of the Use of Cognitive Apprenticeship

In response to rapid changes in the pharmacy profession, a university pharmacy school offers a program to teach community pharmacists how to clinically assess patients' needs and provide patient guidance. The five-phase process is as follows:

Phase 1. Watched by community pharmacists-learners, a pharmacist-model assesses patients' needs and provides patient guidance. The model's *articulation* includes reasons for the questions asked, decisions made, and language used as well as the potential difficulties to avoid. The model explains *domain-specific heuristics* to improve compliance with medication instructions, for example, instructing patients to put a week's supply of tablets in a container with separate divisions for each day.

Phase 2. After observing the model, the pharmacists-learners approximate patient assessment and guidance procedures under *scaffolded* conditions. *Scaffolding* is provided by a computerized drug interaction program and close monitoring by the model. After assessing patients' needs and making guidance decisions, learners discuss patient cases with the pharmacist-model, who *coaches* them, offering suggestions for obtaining additional information. The learners *reflect* on the differences between the model's approach and their approaches. The model offers *remediation* as necessary.

Phase 3. The pharmacists-learners return to their practices and assess selected patients, contacting the pharmacist-model prior to initiating interventions. The model validates appropriate decisions and provides *remediation* for inadequate decisions. The guidance gradually *fades* as the learners show that they are functioning well.

Phase 4. The learners work independently, assessing and guiding patients in their own ways within specified limits acceptable to the profession and society. The pharmacist-model provides assistance only on request.

Phase 5. The pharmacist-model and the learners discuss the generalizability of what was learned in the cognitive apprenticeship experience to relevant learning experiences that are currently available or that can be developed.

Implementing Cognitive Apprenticeship

Crucial to implementation of cognitive apprenticeship are the steps of selecting the type of situation that best matches learner needs, choosing the model to be used, and facilitating the experience. Continuing educators can play a key role in the facilitation as well as in the selection of the situation and model. The latter is usually done in consultation with practitioners in the profession.

Selecting the Situation. A situation is a relative position or combination of circumstances at a certain moment. A situation can also be a critical, trying, or unusual state of affairs. Professionals are expected to function in ways that are predictable, stable, and coordinated with the efforts of others, while doing so in ways that work well for them within acceptable limits defined by the profession and society. The professions have different degrees of tolerance for variability, but no occupation has professionalized without defining recurring situations and acceptable ways to deal with them (Ruesch, 1975). Knowledge of how to handle a particular type of situation is consensually validated by a profession more or less formally through certification tests, legal decisions, journals' refereeing processes, discussions at professional conferences, and other formal and informal gatherings.

As professions develop, they identify certain types of situations as well defined and others as moderately well defined. All other situations addressed by practitioners in the profession are considered ill-defined. A situation is well defined when there is wide agreement in a profession about how to understand and deal with it. A situation is moderately well defined when there are two or more widely agreed-on ways of understanding and dealing with it, and there is consensus about how to select among the alternatives. An ill-defined situation is one that cannot be dealt with as responsibly and adequately as a well-defined or moderately well defined situation is handled.

In selecting a type of situation for a cognitive apprenticeship experience, the continuing educator should consider the typology of situations shown in Table 4.1. In this matrix, there is a progression from well-defined, simple, and risk-free situations to ill-defined, complex, and risky ones. Practitioners in the field can assist the educator in defining the elements of the matrix. Moving to higher numbers on the matrix means moving up in the "zone of problematicity" (Elshout, 1987). This can be done by (1) going from well-defined to moderately well defined to ill-defined situations and/or (2) increasing levels of risk incurred in trying to understand and deal with such situations. Cognitive apprenticeship should begin with the number immediately higher than the highest that learners can already handle for any particular type of activity. Generally, learners should master lower number levels before going to higher ones. Instruction can continue sequentially as far as time and the learners' ability and motivation permit.

The higher the number on the matrix, the greater the probability that cognitive apprenticeship, as opposed to other forms of instruction, will be helpful. Nevertheless, cognitive apprenticeship may be the most efficient way of learning in the case of lower numbers on the matrix.

Choosing the Model. The choice of an appropriate professional to do the modeling is important. Because learners learn best when they identify with the person instructing them, the models should be similar in age, cultural background, and outlook to the learners. Models must understand and deal with the particular type of situation at a level to which the learners can appropriately strive. Cognitive apprenticeship can teach proficient performance to those not yet proficient in understanding and dealing with ill-defined, risky, and complex situations. Proficiency means the ability to do the activity in a minimally acceptable way, on one's own,

Table 4.1. Types of Situations That Professionals Seek to Understand and Deal With Satisfactorily

	Order of Situation		
Extent of Risk to the Learner or Others	Well-Defined	Moderately Well Defined	Ill-Defined
High	7	8	9
	4	5	6
Low	1	2	3

Source: Based on Johnson and Farmer, 1989.

while avoiding identifiable pitfalls (Lippert and Farmer, 1984). Cognitive apprenticeship can also teach expertise to professionals who are already proficient in understanding and dealing with a specific type of situation. The educator must choose the appropriate model for each situation: Proficient performance should be taught by proficient models; expert performance by expert models whose expertise does not depend mainly on personal idiosyncracies. Models are typically chosen through nominations by practicing professionals.

Models vary in their ability to transmit robust, reliable knowledge. The best model is someone who can demonstrate how to perform the task in a progressive, consensually validated way and can articulate reasons for actions based not only on experience but also on application of previously learned and/or sought out generalizations from relevant professional fields, sciences, and disciplines. The model's ability to draw on a wide variety of sources enhances the flexibility and generalizability of what is learned.

Cognitive apprenticeship can sometimes be used even when a field has no consensually validated way(s) of dealing with a type of situation. Practitioners who understand and deal with such situations may be used as models. A more effective approach is to use an anomaly-based workshop (Farmer, 1990) to generate consensually validated knowledge-in-action. In an anomaly-based workshop, professionals with experience and at least partial success in understanding and dealing with particular situations share what they have learned and recommend approaches that can be used in practice. Workshop participants may subsequently become cognitive apprenticeship models.

Facilitating Cognitive Apprenticeship. In addition to their key role in selection of situations and models, continuing educators may, first, facilitate the cognitive apprenticeship by helping the model(s) and learners articulate thoughts that occur during performance, describe thought processes, summarize internal speech and what is sensed, and explain the reasons for particular types of thinking (Ericsson and Simon, 1984). Models and learners should be asked to think aloud while they perform, if this does not interfere with performance. The procedure of asking initially for descriptions and then for explanations may help encourage models to "tell it like it is" instead of "telling it like it ought to be." Second, continuing educators may act as models if they have recent experience in understanding and dealing with the real-life situations. And, third, they may act as resources, discussing the situations and offering suggestions from the perspective of their relevant scientific or other knowledge.

What Makes Cognitive Apprenticeship Effective?

The fundamental premise of the cognitive apprenticeship model is *situated cognition* (Vygotsky, 1978). Knowledge is created and made meaningful by the context in which it is acquired. Its use is not merely a matter of pattern recognition but rather is action-oriented (Resnick, 1989b). "Ideas become clarified and personalized during use; and have only limited meaning prior to use. The context of use affects the way an idea is understood" (Eraut, 1985, p. 117). Cognitive apprenticeship facilitates development of appropriate learner schemas by embedding the learning of practical knowledge in its natural context and having models make explicit the knowledge and attitudes associated with their behavior. This approach is especially valuable because it supplements standard modes of teaching, it bridges practice and theory in potentially dangerous situations, and it demystifies practice knowledge.

Teaching What Is Normally Not Taught but Is Needed for Effective, Efficient Practice. In cognitive apprenticeship, a model describes and demonstrates examples, metaphors, practical principles, and rules of thumb used in professional practice (Cervero, 1992). These can include ideals generalized from experience that is informed by theoretical knowledge and sensitivity to contextual clues that modify behavior in ways appropriate to the specific circumstances (McAlpine, 1991). Also included may be ways to apply knowledge from relevant sciences, disciplines, and applied fields or ways to use this knowledge perspectively, "looking through it" as one looks through sunglasses.

Avoidance of Danger. Cognitive apprenticeship uses the processes known as "bootstrapping" and "finessing" (Resnick, 1989a, pp. 3–4) to help learners take advantage of the model's knowledge and assistance in order to understand and deal with certain types of situations before they have all of the necessary knowledge and skills. The model's experience helps them avoid danger and errors. For example, a pilot performs a new maneuver assisted by an experienced pilot model who intervenes if necessary. The experience of performing gives the learners knowledge-in-action and helps them bridge the gap between theory and practice.

Demystification. Cognitive apprenticeship can demystify an occupation and empower learners by allowing personal and professional knowledge-in-action to be seen and discussed to the extent possible and feasible. For example, an opportunity is provided to learn the type of practical knowledge that cannot be fully described in writing because it is essentially nonverbal, such as a change in tone of voice or a certain facial expression. It also encourages models to verbalize three types of reflection important to practice in that they reveal decision processes not normally taught: reflection-for-practice, reflection-in-practice, and reflection-on-practice (McAlpine, 1991).

Conclusion

Cognitive apprenticeship contributes to the field by giving continuing professional educators an additional tool to help professionals learn to perform satisfactorily in keeping with the expectations of professions and society. Sometimes professionals can understand and deal with situations incurred in practice by using common sense, logic, intuition, and/or the application of general principles. When these approaches are insufficient, self-directed learning and/or traditional learning devices such as workshops and short courses may provide the additional knowledge, attitudes, or skills needed to understand and deal satisfactorily with situations. Unfortunately, these methods are often insufficient for learning to understand and deal satisfactorily with ill-defined, risky, and complex situations.

A switch from these methods to cognitive apprenticeship is likely to be helpful when (1) the task to be learned must be performed in a manner acceptable to society and the profession rather than in whatever way that learners work out and (2) the task can be modeled and then practiced by professionals under scaffolded conditions. Use of cognitive apprenticeship is particularly appropriate when (1) learners need a form of instruction that is more effective and efficient than self-directed learning or didactic instruction to help them learn to understand and deal satisfactorily with a specific type of situation, (2) there is a realistic, low tolerance for error or risk, and/or (3) learners have failed to learn adequately through other methods.

References

Brown, J. S., Collins, A., and Duguid, P. "Situated Cognition and the Culture of Learning." *Educational Researcher,* 1989, *18,* 32–42.

Buckmaster, A., Farmer, J. A., Jr., and LeGrand, B. "Cognitive Apprenticeship: Implications for Cognitive Reframing in Counseling." *Illinois Association for Counseling and Development Quarterly,* 1990, *119,* 2–11.

Cervero, R. M. "Professional Practice, Learning, and Continuing Education: An Integrated Perspective." *International Journal of Lifelong Education,* 1992, *11* (2), 91–101.

Collins, A., Brown, J. S., and Newman, S. E. "Cognitive Apprenticeship: Teaching the Craft of Reading, Writing, and Mathematics." In L. B. Resnick (ed.), *Knowing, Learning, and Instruction: Essays in Honor of Robert Glaser.* Hillsdale, N.J.: Erlbaum, 1989.

Elshout, J. J. "Problem-Solving and Education." In E. DeCorte, H. Lodewijks, H. R. Parmenties, and P. Spau (eds.), *Learning and Instruction: European Research and International Context.* Vol. 1. Oxford, England: Pergamon Press/Leuven University Press, 1987.

Eraut, M. "Knowledge Creation and Knowledge Use in Professional Contexts." *Studies in Higher Education,* 1985, *10* (2), 117–133.

Ericsson, K., and Simon, H. *Protocol Analysis: Verbal Reports as Data.* Cambridge, Mass.: MIT Press, 1984.

Farmer, J. A., Jr. "The Three-Foci Model and Its Implications for CME." In *Continuing Medical Education: Measurement Issues on Trial.* Proceedings of the 22nd Annual Conference on Research in Medical Education. Washington, D.C.: Association of American Medical Colleges, 1983.

Farmer, J. A., Jr. "Provocative Issues." In W. B. Leadbetter, J. A. Buckwalter, and S. L. Gordon (eds.), *Sports-Induced Inflammation: Clinical and Basic Science Concepts.* Park Ridge, Ill.: American Academy of Orthopaedic Surgeons, 1990.

Farmer, J. A., Jr., Buckmaster, A., and LeGrand, B. "Useful Knowledge for Adult and Continuing Education." *Setting the Pace,* 1989, *4* (1), 3–7.

Farmer, J. A., Jr., Lippert, F. G., and Schafer, M. "Making Orthopaedic Educators Interactive, Problem-Oriented, and on Target." In R. E. Eilert (ed.), *Instructional Course Lectures.* Vol. 41. Park Ridge, Ill.: American Academy of Orthopaedic Surgeons, 1991.

Farmer, J. A., Jr., Schafer, M., and Lippert, F. G. "Physician-Educator Interactions." *Lifelong Learning: An Omnibus of Practice and Research,* 1983, 7 (2), 14–15, 25, 28.

Gist, M. "The Influence of Training Method on Self-Efficacy and Idea Generation Among Managers." *Personnel Psychology,* 1989, *42,* 787–803.

Jarvis, P. *Adult Learning in the Social Context.* London, England: Croom-Helm, 1987.

Johnson, A. L., and Farmer, J. A., Jr. "Teaching Veterinary Surgery in the Operating Room." *Journal of Veterinary Medical Education,* 1989, *16* (1), 10–12.

Lippert, F. G., and Farmer, J. A., Jr. *Psychomotor Skills in Orthopaedic Surgery.* Baltimore, Md.: Williams and Wilkins, 1984.

McAlpine, L. "Narrative Pedagogy: Bridging Theory and Practice Using Learner Narrative to Develop a Personal Notion of Practice." Paper presented at the conference of the International Society for Educational Biography, Toronto, Ontario, Canada, April 1991.

Meichenbaum, D. *Cognitive Behavior Modification.* New York: Plenum, 1977.

Perry, M. A., and Furukawa, M. J. "Modeling Methods." In F. K. Kanfer and A. P. Goldstein (eds.), *Helping People Change: A Textbook of Methods.* (2nd ed.) Elmsford, N.Y.: Pergamon Press, 1980.

Prestine, N., and LeGrand, B. "Cognitive Learning Theory and the Preparation of Educational Administrators: Implications for Practice and Policy." *Educational Administration Quarterly,* 1991, *27* (1), 61–89.

Resnick, L. B. "Learning in School and Out." *Educational Researcher,* 1987, *16,* 13–20.

Resnick, L. B. "Introduction." In L. B. Resnick (ed.), *Knowing, Learning, and Instruction: Essays in Honor of Robert Glaser.* Hillsdale, N.J.: Erlbaum, 1989a.

Resnick, L. B. (ed.). *Knowing, Learning, and Instruction: Essays in Honor of Robert Glaser.* Hillsdale, N.J.: Erlbaum, 1989b.

Ruesch, J. *Knowledge in Action.* New York: Jason Aronson, 1975.

Vygotsky, L. S. "Mind in Society." In M. Cole, V. John-Steiner, S. Scribner, and E. Souberman (eds. and trans.), *Mind in Society: The Development of Higher Psychological Processes.* Cambridge, Mass.: Harvard University Press, 1978.

West, C. K., Farmer, J. A., Jr., and Wolff, P. M. *Instructional Design: Implications from Cognitive Science.* Englewood Cliffs, N.J.: Prentice Hall, 1991.

James A. Farmer, Jr., is associate professor of continuing education, University of Illinois, Urbana-Champaign.

Annette Buckmaster is a consultant to the Office of Continuing Education, Training and Development, University of Illinois, Urbana-Champaign.

Barbara LeGrand is associate director of continuing education at the College of Pharmacy, University of Kentucky, Lexington.

What is a learning organization? How can the capabilities of a large complex organization be developed in a way that delivers quality business results? This chapter follows the journey of Imperial Oil Resources Ltd. of Canada as it addresses both of these questions.

Capability Development at Imperial Oil Resources Ltd.

David Ellerington, Victoria J. Marsick,
Kathleen Dechant

At one time in its recent history, the oil industry was fairly stable and predictable, leading to standard ways of thinking about success in the industry. The industry has now become as volatile as telecommunications, retailing, or computer technology. Indeed, the current question being faced by the oil industry is whether it will be able to survive, and in what form.

Over the past decade, Imperial Oil Resources Ltd. of Canada (formerly known as Esso Resources Canada Ltd.) responded to and, in many instances, anticipated the changing environment of the late 1980s and early 1990s. It is tempting to convince ourselves that each step was deliberately taken to enhance the company's ability to learn and command its own destiny, but this was not the case. The rationale for each step was prompted by external and internal business pressures. Some of the steps were deliberate, but many evolved without much conscious thought or planning. Looking back, we can see each step as having contributed to a learning culture. Like the weaving of a tapestry, each thread, while colorful, may not in itself look significant. Once woven, however, it is possible to recognize that the final product is different from the simple sum of these threads, although perhaps not as valuable without each and every thread.

Limitations of Training

Over the years, Imperial Oil Resources has actively provided a range of technical and nontechnical training courses for all levels of employees.

Undoubtedly, this training had a positive impact on the organization, both directly by the development of skills and knowledge and indirectly by the development of shared corporate values. However, training has not always ensured transfer of learning outcomes back to the workplace. One reason can be traced to the general nature of training, which should be viewed as only one way to enhance learning. Training usually takes place in a classroom and is facilitated by trainers, controlled by experts, and structured or deliberately designed. Learning, on the other hand, takes place whenever problems or dilemmas are encountered, is facilitated (when it is) by educators and controlled by learners, and may not be very well structured or designed at all.

As Marsick and Watkins (1990) and Dechant (1990) point out, learning requires a different skill set from that of training. To be effective at learning, employees must learn continuously from their experience. When learning from experience, we often make errors because our interpretations may be based on faulty reasoning, personal projections, and taken-for-granted beliefs that have not been tested. Even if employees become effective at learning from experience, the culture of an organization may make it difficult to learn or to act on that learning when employees are back on the job. This means that individuals cannot benefit from learning, and thus the organization does not benefit.

The transfer of training is a long-standing issue. To this is added a new challenge: the need to create learning organizations in which not only do individuals learn continuously but also the organization learns by capturing individual learning gains, sharing them among employees, and setting up channels to translate them into new policies, procedures, and other ways of doing business. The changes in learning initiated by Imperial Oil Resources illustrate a journey toward the learning organization (Ellerington, 1991).

Early Experiments with Strategies to Support Learning

Traditionally, Imperial Oil Resources offered employees well-designed, intensive, internal courses on a range of subjects that had either been identified through routine needs analysis or had been recognized as valuable to the company. These courses were generally staffed by internal company trainers. However, in 1981, a move was made to provide more custom-designed workshops in order to meet needs specific to individual departments and work units. The intention was to take the training into the workplace and involve all members of a work unit in the learning experience. The premise was that this workplace involvement would increase the likelihood of a commitment to changed behavior by all work unit members and, therefore, the likelihood of a more sustained result.

While customized training provided many examples of success, in 1988, the Human Resources Department decided to create a new strategy to support learning in recognition of an increased need to emphasize ownership by the employee for his or her own learning, the critical need for a supportive learning environment, and the linkage between learning and business initiatives. Training was not abandoned; well-designed activities were continued, as needed, through a range of in-house courses. At the same time, the trainer's role began to be redefined as a learning consultant, creating confusion for both the learning consultant and the clients about what such a person does if he or she does not give courses. The bottom line, however, was that learning was to be more integrated into the daily challenges that individuals and teams faced as they did their work. The outcome was to encourage substantive breakthrough changes in thinking and in working.

Learning consultants were assigned to company departments to work with line managers to identify learning needs in support of business strategies. Individual employee development was assisted by issuing to each employee, by way of the supervisor, a self-service guide to learning. The guide took employees through a step-by-step process to develop an individualized plan of formal and informal learning. The guide was supported by a learning resources directory and a learning journal. While this approach did raise the awareness and interest of employees in their own development, it was not enough to leave the responsibility to employees without more structured guidance.

Opportunities for Employee Development

The merger of Imperial Oil Resources and Texaco Canada in 1989 created many opportunities to build learning into work challenges. Approximately fifty "synergy" teams were created to make recommendations on how specific issues regarding the merger should be resolved. Issues ranged from the macrodesign of structures, systems, and policies down to detailed identification of individual jobs and who should fill them. Each synergy team consisted of six to ten employees from various positions and levels in both organizations.

Each synergy team was provided with a coach. Everyone participated in a chartering and capability development session to launch the effort. Learning was built into team meetings, with time provided to reflect on and share learning. "Poster-booth" sessions took place where members of synergy teams, stakeholders, and other employees could visit displays on office walls that illustrated the output of different teams and catalyzed feedback to the team. These sessions made each team's learnings accessible to others. They clearly conveyed to employees throughout the company what people were learning and how they were going about this process. As a result of synergy team experiences, team members began to be more effective at articulating and challenging assumptions, seeking a variety of approaches to tasks, and using resources. During these capability development sessions teams worked on real issues as they developed their capabilities, and this was a critical dimension in the process. The phrase frequently used to describe participants' experience was "using live ammunition." Another important consequence of this real-time learning was that the organization learned as well. Teams were expected to become adept at changing their learning through the organization.

The intensity and urgency of the merger provided an opportunity to examine a philosophy proposed by consultant Charles Krone. Krone has been accused of, and heralded for, operating on an "esoteric plane" in his attempts to offer practical applications of systems thinking to the design of organizations. The fundamental premise of his theory is that knowledge and technology are advancing at such a rapid rate that an organization is ill-served by focusing its energy on acquiring and advancing technical expertise; the more valuable human asset is the capacity to think, to reason, and to improve on the many levels of activity in an organization. Hence, the essence of Krone's consultation is directed at the depth, comprehension, and deliberation of thought.

Human resources staff utilized aspects of Krone's philosophy to support development of the variety of teams involved in the merger. The concept of capability development goes beyond the simple accumulation of knowledge and skill. Capability development begins with the inner self, as advocated by Senge (1990) in relation to personal mastery. Individuals use knowledge or skills when they are satisfied that their actions are consistent with their beliefs and values, and that they can make choices based on their commitments. They carry through on actions when they are self-confident and have staying power to achieve goals even when the going is rough.

The concept of capability development showed merit during the merger, by both its refreshing approach and its attention to integration into the work. A working definition emerged to describe it: "The development and utilization of the critical skills, abilities, attitudes, and commitments to achieve business success and to do this in continuously improving ways."

Discussion Paper: A Strategy for Capability Development

Past the initial stages of the merger between Imperial Oil Resources and Texaco Canada, the need developed to clarify and agree on the future role and direction for capability development. At that point in 1990, a discussion paper was written for use with a cross-section of employees, including vice presidents and general managers. The paper laid out the rationale for a capability development strategy in terms of business results, offered a vision of the company five years hence, and identified factors that would be critical to achieving the vision. The purpose of the paper was not to propose the "right answer" but rather to stimulate discussion that would lead to commitment to the strategy. The paper contained three areas of focus: organizationwide, divisional, and individual capabilities.

Organizationwide Capabilities. While the selection of the three capabilities was critical, it was equally important to gain commitment to the selection and stay the course in consistently developing the chosen three across the company. In the past, the Resources Division had a tendency to introduce new programs without always following through to full implementation. Sometimes this result proved appropriate, but at other times the tendency led to confusion in the organization and dilution of the benefits of what otherwise had been a well-designed and fruitful intervention.

The three capabilities identified as most supportive of the company's corporate vision were as follows:

Rigorous Selection of Essential Work. Organizations have become leaner and demands on employees greater. General Electric has pioneered in a strategy called "Workout" to help reduce workload while ensuring that priorities are met. The Resources Division at Imperial Oil adapted a similar goal in this first capability. To face the challenging environment, the staff needed to distinguish between work that was critical to success and work that was interesting, even useful, but not essential. To carry out this analysis, they formed a steering committee, which, aided by an external consulting firm specializing in adjusting the work force to correspond to the workload, was able to develop a direction and framework for the division's actions. The methodology used in some ways reflected the merger process. Action teams of five to seven employees studied the work carried out across the company and recommended where work could be eliminated. This process formed a basis for an ongoing shift in mindset, which encouraged all employees to challenge whether every aspect of their work was essential to business success.

Continuous Improvement. A corporate framework was developed as a means to focus attention on continuous improvement of the company's work. A team of continuous improvement facilitators was established, each of whom was assigned to a particular business unit. The framework addressed issues of customer focus, work process improvement, and supportive work environment, in addition to the issue of essential work.

Development of Leaders Who Can Make a Business Difference. This need is being approached on two levels. For middle managers and first-level supervisors, a formal program, Leadership-in-Action, has been established. This program is structured around action-learning principles (Marsick and Cederholm, 1988) and provides a core of content around leadership behaviors, while simultaneously providing participants with skills and a framework in which to learn from their own experience. Participants form learning teams for the four-month duration of the program and meet, together with a learning facilitator, at regular intervals to review their experiences and new learning. In addition, assignments are structured for development purposes. Individual executive capability needs are being matched with available jobs and a learning support structure.

Divisional Capabilities. Each division has a business plan or a roadmap that is linked to the overall corporate plan. The division identifies the specific capabilities required by its employees to ensure that the plan is accomplished. These capabilities are wide and varied.

Having prioritized its perceived list of essential capabilities, the division's leadership team agrees on the capabilities requiring development. Frequently, this action phase moves from the broad divisional level down to individual work units. It is important that the behaviors, and related capabilities required by the work unit leaders and members, are identified by the work unit itself, and that there is commitment to the process. Once these capabilities are agreed on and the high-leverage development opportunities highlighted, then attention can be paid to the processes used to achieve development. These processes may include formal training courses, clinics, conferences, coaching, or mentoring. In many cases, all that is required is the provision of information to employees so that they can understand the work unit's goals and how they can contribute to the achievement of those goals.

Individual Capabilities. Traditionally, emphasis is placed on individual, as opposed to group, learning, often in the context of job and career development. The capability development strategy built on this emphasis by helping individuals develop their personal capabilities as effective learners. In addition, consideration was given to enhancing the work environment to support the occurrence of learning.

Pulling the Strategy All Together

To face the challenge of creating companywide alignment, and to avoid taking away ownership from the individual divisions, a capability development cooperative was formed, consisting of nearly one hundred employees from all levels and divisions of the company. The members joined on a volunteer basis to enhance capability development within their business units and to establish alignment of members' efforts so that divisions can enhance business results in consonance with corporate strategy. The term *cooperative* reflects a group of individuals who share a common interest, are committed to success, and expect to take away a product of personal value.

From their initial experience with the cooperative, the human resources development staff learned to be in a position to offer solid successes and methodology. While the energy of and commitment to the cooperative was high, members were looking for someone else to show proof of the practical results of capability development. As everyone was still a beginner, these successes had not yet materialized. After a year of useful ground work, it was decided to suspend the group and focus attention on three to four individual capability development projects. Once practical experience has been gained, the cooperative will reconvene and build on the learning from these divisions.

Learning as a Capability

The change in conceptual strategy from training to learning, and from learning to capability development, has been a difficult journey for human resources staff. The heart of the learning strategy is based on the task of building awareness that learning stems primarily from business purposes and plans established by the company and by each individual division. The center of attention is the business of the business.

Due to difficult economic times in early 1992, which resulted in company downsizing and layoffs of human resources staff, those remaining have had to refocus their efforts on providing the essential training programs. Until that downsizing occurred, efforts continued to capture the opportunities for revisioning the function and role of human resources staff, opportunities made possible by the merger of Imperial Oil Resources and Texaco Canada. So as not to lose the valuable lessons gained, the journey and its implications are described here.

Human resources staff moved away from a primary reliance on centrally provided formal workshops and courses, although they were still available and used when a need existed. Training was reallocated to the business units, and human resources staff assisted as these units attempted to run their own programs. Individuals were expected to play a greater role in identifying their learning needs and in selecting ways to meet these needs.

As a further move toward integrating training and formal learning into the work unit, "just-in-time" learning was introduced into the divisions. A wide range of clinics and short learning experiences were made available in response to needs as they arose.

Attention was also paid to the task of more effectively integrating learning with ongoing work challenges. For example, people often took time in meetings to reflect on what they were learning and how that would help in future tasks. Aids were developed to support people as they confronted new challenges. For example, the tool kit developed for the synergy teams was used by many of the teams and networks throughout the company. Project groups called on the services of facilitators to help them when they were blocked. The capability development cooperative sponsored short, informal clinics targeted at brushups of skills in specific areas identified by divisions. These clinics were staffed by people within the company who were identified as good resources.

Lessons Learned

In reflecting on the past few years' experience at a capability development strategy meeting in the company, staff identified several key lessons. First, without a doubt, training and development of individuals is essential to an organization, but by itself it is frequently insufficient. The major roadblock is transferring what the individuals learn in the classroom to the day-to-day business of the job.

Second, there is a greater readiness to connect learning to the business when the capability development process is owned by the work unit and driven by the business strategy and when many of the employees of the unit are involved in creating the strategy.

Third, organization members as individuals are generally quick to acknowledge the value of learning in the workplace and recognize that the organization should be able to extract lessons from experience. However, in practice, work groups, as well as individuals, are frequently so eager to move into action that they fail to dedicate sufficient time to critically reflect on their experience. Often, they have not developed adequate personal skills in learning nor have they established processes that enable effective learning to occur.

It seems clear that for organizational learning to occur, the formal systems and processes must support a "learning attitude." For example, the business planning process should serve as a means of reflection on lessons learned from experience as well as a forum for goal setting.

Conclusion

What does this chapter offer to those who are trying to facilitate professional ways of knowing and learning? One of the most obvious lessons is that plans and innovations can be abruptly ended when the energy and resources of an organization are required for survival rather than development. Just as the business plan can be used to drive innovations in human resources development, it can also eliminate those innovations. However, while acknowledging this reality, what other lessons can be gleaned from this experiment in enhancing learning in an organization?

First, the experience of the Resources Division suggests that employees at all levels of the organization must be considered potential "professionals" to the extent that their work increasingly draws on a specialized knowledge base as well as a level of independent judgment reserved for professionals in the past. Second, learning cannot be confined to the classroom because if it is not continuous, it is not of maximum use, either to individuals or to the organization. Third, we know little about how to enhance continuous learning, but it is clear that individual intrinsic motivation and commitment are essential, and that learning consultants must work with people close to the site of their experiences to maximize learning gains. Continuous learning requires new roles as learning consultants, and new skills as proactive learners. Finally, the organizational norms, values, beliefs, and culture play a significant role in ensuring that learning takes place and that it is shared, rewarded, and used to enhance individual and organization gains.

The experiences of Imperial Oil Resources Ltd. have illustrated the lack of any clearcut prescription to develop the capabilities required to meet an organization's business needs. Rather, the process is one of experimentation, critical reflection, and learning from the experience. While it is easy to become frustrated and disillusioned, perseverance can bring forth remarkable results.

References

Ellerington, D. *Creating Companywide Capability: What Managers Need to Know and Do.* Developing Tomorrow's Managers, Report No. 984. New York: Conference Board, 1991.

Dechant, K. "Knowing How to Learn: The Neglected Management Ability." *Journal of Management Development,* 1990, 9 (4), 40–49.

Marsick, V. J., and Cederholm, L. "Developing Leadership in International Managers—An Urgent Challenge!" *Columbia Journal of World Business,* 1988, 23 (4), 3–11.

Marsick, V. J., and Watkins, K. E. *Informal and Incidental Learning in the Workplace.* New York: Routledge & Kegan Paul, 1990.

Senge, P. *The Fifth Discipline: The Art and Practice of the Learning Organization.* New York: Doubleday, 1990.

DAVID ELLERINGTON is a capability development consultant at Imperial Oil Resources Ltd. During his twenty years as a training and learning professional, he has worked in many parts of the Exxon worldwide circuit. He was a member of the capability development team that supported the merger between Imperial Oil Resources Ltd. and Texaco Canada.

VICTORIA J. MARSICK is associate professor of adult and continuing education at Teachers College, Columbia University in New York City. She currently consults with both the private and public sectors on the design of learning organizations and training approaches.

KATHLEEN DECHANT is assistant professor of management, School of Business Administration, University of Connecticut, Stamford.

*In some situations, the potential for informal learning may be not
only in the experiences of the workplace, but also in the type of work
relationship in effect at the time the experiences occur.*

Professional Learning Through Workplace Partnerships

Barbara K. Lovin

Continued learning within the professions is not only a mandate of many
certifying agencies but a necessity if practicing professionals are to maintain competence in fields where obsolescence can occur rapidly and with
devastating consequences. While formalized instruction plays a role in
this continued learning, evidence suggests that individuals learn as much
or more through informal means in workplace settings (Carnevale and
Goldstein, 1983). The workplace, then, is a significant learning resource.
Yet, the multidimensional nature of informal learning and the contextual
diversity of the workplace are such that adult educators have yet to fully
capitalize on this learning resource.

A qualitative study of a group of health care practitioners was undertaken to provide a better understanding of the ways in which professionals learn informally. The study was based on the belief that such an
understanding can provide insight into ways to enhance learning, both
formal and informal, in the workplace setting. This case study was
conducted with a public, countywide provider of emergency medical
services in a southeastern state. Of the fifty-six paramedics employed by
this service, twenty-three paramedics, twenty males and three females
with one to nine years' experience, self-selected for the study. Quotations
are from the primary data sources of this study: (1) a critical incident that
asked participants to write about a particular challenge each had faced
on the job, (2) semistructured interviews with each paramedic, and (3)
extended observations of three of them within their work environment.
Paramedics are emergency care providers who offer basic and advanced
life support to acutely ill or injured patients in the prehospital setting.

Marsick and Watkins (1987) identify job assignments and workplace

NEW DIRECTIONS FOR ADULT AND CONTINUING EDUCATION, no. 55, Fall 1992 © Jossey-Bass Publishers

relationships as important sources of informal learning among all types of workers. For these paramedics, job assignments and workplace relationships are affected by contextual features of the work environment that appear to impact significantly on the informal learning occurring there. These practitioners operate in a world of discrete events, namely, calls for emergency medical assistance that usually begin with a phone call to 911 and end when documentation of the event is completed by a paramedic. In addition, these paramedics perform their job assignments not as individuals but in concert with a partner with whom they live and work for periods of up to twenty-four hours at a time. In this type of environment, as opposed to independent modes of informal learning, workplace relationships and job assignments have a direct bearing on one another and, in the process, affect the informal learning potential of the workplace.

Learning from Experience

Learning from experience emerges as the dominant mode of informal learning in this workplace setting. The paramedics use the experiences of the workplace to better understand the nature of the job, the organization, themselves, and those with whom they work. They believe that "experience is the best teacher" and that "the best learning is doing." They report learning during the actual performance of the tasks of the job, learning from mistakes made in the completion of a job assignment, learning through reflection while documenting their job performance, and learning from the experiences of others through listening to stories.

Based on consideration of how learning from experience occurs among this group of health care professionals, two findings appear significant. First, it is the nonroutine experiences of the job that are recognized by the paramedics as the primary sources of learning in this setting (Argyris and Schön, 1974). These unusual experiences are not just the challenges of the critical incidents, they are also the "unique calls, funny calls," and the "classic calls that would go down in the record book." The learning involved is sometimes discovered while reflecting on a job assignment: "You're writing down whatever therapy you did, and then you write down what it did and you say, 'Remember that!' " Nonroutine experiences may also be the mistakes that make a routine call unusual. "I probably wouldn't have even remembered that call had I not made a mistake." They may even be routine calls in unusual circumstances: "This guy swerved to miss a squirrel." Although all these nonroutine calls officially conclude with the submission of call documentation, they are often resurrected, for it is also the nonroutine experiences of the job that are the incidents most often shared through storytelling: "Did you hear about . . . ?"

The second significant finding suggests that what might be a nonroutine job experience for some paramedics may be routine for others. The determining factor appears to be the type of partnership in effect at the time of the experience. Therefore, the potential for learning is not only in the nature of the experience itself but in how the experience is viewed in light of the partnership in effect at the time.

A Process for Learning from Experience. The strategies employed by these paramedics in learning from experience—storytelling, reflection, mistakes, and performance of the tasks associated with the job—seem to describe a four-phase process for how that learning occurs.

Acquisition Phase. In this phase, potential learning experiences are acquired. While paramedics encounter these experiences most often during performance of the job, the term *acquired* is chosen because of evidence that significant learning occurs as a result of listening to the experiences of others. Storytelling or "trading war stories" used as a strategy for acquiring potential learning experiences suggests that, in contrast to Kolb's (1984) experiential learning model, personal involvement is not necessary for an experience to be acquired and the potential to exist for significant learning to occur.

Formulation Phase. In this phase, acquired experiences are filtered through the sieve of past experiences. This is the point at which acquired experiences separate into routine and nonroutine. A perceived need to know, in the sense that the paramedic does not have sufficient knowledge or skills to adequately address the situation, seems to be the trap that designates an experience as nonroutine and places it in line for consideration during subsequent phases of the learning process. "We knew we were in for a mess because there was a truck halfway on a car and the car was hanging over the bridge. We were sort of stumped." Jarvis (1987) says that experiences must be meaningful to individuals if they are to be learning situations. A perceived need to know, though not always so dramatic, suggests that an experience has meaning.

Learning occurs in the formulation phase, but it is implicit. It is the nature of the job of the paramedic that learning from experience may never become explicit because the situation may never arise where the new learning can be tried out. Yet, in acknowledging a need to know, the participants in this study demonstrate an awareness that the potential exists for new learning to eventually be vital to their job performance.

Experimentation Phase. Learning, while not yet explicit, is further developed during the experimentation phase, where learning, acquired from personal experience or the experiences of others, is tried out. This experimentation often involves risk taking as new learning is tested against organizational norms, practice standards, personal beliefs, or existing relationships. In certain instances, as during medical emergencies, experimentation may follow directly upon the recognition of a need to know. "At each step we would talk about it and say, 'Well, if we did it this way what would happen?' " At other times, experimentation is delayed until appropriate conditions exist: "On the way back from a call we critique it and say, 'Next time we'll try something a little bit different.' "

Confirmation Phase. Experimentation can lead to a rejection of the learning as dysfunctional or to a fully developed expression of new learning that then becomes a part of the repertoire of the paramedic. This confirmation of learning is the fourth and final phase of the process of learning from experience. It is responsible for removing from future acquired experiences the perceived need to know, for it is through the learning process that the unusual becomes routine.

It appears that the paramedics recognize that the process of learning from experience is not final. What has been learned becomes part of the filter for formulating newly acquired experiences. This kind of recognition appears important given the demands on workplace learning presented by the rapid change and increasing complexity of the professional's work environment.

Relationships as Learning Experiences

Paramedics report using a variety of relationships within the workplace setting as resources for learning. Work with a partner is the relationship that provides the most significant learning opportunities. This point is confirmed in a study by Marsick and Watkins (1990), who found that professionals are more likely to learn from peers.

Partner Interactions. In the study reported here, four types of partner interactions are apparent. The first and most common of these, long-term partnerships where the partners consider themselves equals, is often described as "two people that act as one." Participants recognize that in the development of this type of partnership, learning goes beyond that necessary to perform the job. "You learn about each other . . . mannerisms, philosophy, stuff like that." When this partnership develops, the effectiveness of the team approach to a job assignment results in a response exceeding that which is possible by two individuals acting alone. This "oneness" occurs because the partners pool their knowledge, consult, and accomplish tasks efficiently and effectively.

When the organization pairs two paramedics in a mentor-learner type relationship, a second type of partnership is evident. The relationship is hierarchical rather than collaborative. The mentor is described as a "backbone" for the paramedic learner, and the potential exists for this partnership to exceed the effectiveness of two individuals acting independently. Yet, when the situation warrants, mentors admit that they step in and assume control. When this occurs, and the responsibility for the resolution of the situation falls to an individual rather than to the paramedic team, the effectiveness of the partnership is diminished.

A third type of partnership exists when experienced paramedics are paired for relatively brief periods. Here, there appears to be "no meat" in investing the effort necessary to make the partnership work. Individualism characterizes this type of partnership: "When you get stuck with a different partner, you sort of feel by yourself." The partners approach the job as a series of tasks to be accomplished with little interaction. Although the tasks are completed successfully, the results are less than might be expected from a paramedic team. "There are times when you haven't worked with someone that the call just doesn't seem to flow." The effectiveness of the two individual paramedics is not enhanced by their working together, and this pairing of paramedics invalidates many of the benefits of working with a partner.

The fourth and final type of association, the new partnership, is most often in evidence at the beginning of a long-term partnership. In a new partnership, partners want to consider themselves equals but are reluctant to trust one another. They end up "banging into each other" as each assumes full responsibility for completion of the tasks of the job. Unlike the other three partner interactions, here the whole is always less than the sum of the parts. The partners interfere with one another in the completion of job assignments, and the partnership fails to achieve the potential inherent to the pairing of two qualified paramedics.

Partnerships as Sources of Learning. The development of relationships that serve as sources of workplace learning appears conditional on the development of trust (LaParo, 1989). Trust is central to the development of the long-term partnership but is missing in the other three types of partner interactions. Trust between long-term partners encompasses the right to critique and be critiqued, to question and be questioned, and to disagree. These rights in turn become resources for learning within the partnership that improves the ability of the partners to function as competent professionals together and as part of an organization. In mentor-learner relationships designed specifically for learning, even the most basic of trusts, trust in the ability of one's partner to perform the necessary skills of the job, is not equally present. Evidence suggests that the partnership should be viewed as a less than ideal source for learning team effectiveness and the knowledge necessary to maintain competence.

The potential for learning within the short-term partnership is minimal. Although regarded as equals, the partners are reluctant to trust one another. As a result, the learning in this partnership is primarily individual and centers around performance of the job. The new partnership is necessary if partners are to develop a long-term partnership. New partners want to trust each other, and they recognize this need to learn to trust if the effectiveness of the partnership is to be realized. It is in this pairing that the potential of the partnership as a workplace relationship for learning is evident. The path to the long-term partnership is through the new partnership and it develops through a process best described as learning to partner.

Learning to Partner: Making the Unusual Routine. Learning through workplace relationships and from nonroutine workplace experiences are important modes of informal learning. The findings suggest that the relationships themselves can be the nonroutine experiences. When this occurs, one recognized mode of informal learning, learning from relationships, becomes the event of another recognized mode, learning from nonroutine workplace experience.

In this setting, the principal relationship is the partnership between two paramedics. While the findings characterize four different partner interactions, they also suggest that all but one of these four is a nonroutine experience for the individuals involved. Viewed in this light, there are two categories of partnerships, routine and nonroutine. Only the long-term partnership can be characterized as routine. The study supports the ideas that the long-term partnership has become routine because the paramedic partners have learned to partner and that they learn to partner through the same process by which learning from other workplace experiences is accomplished.

Paramedics recognize as nonroutine the acquired experience of being paired with another individual for the first time. According to the proposed learning process, this recognition implies a need to know. Yet, if one examines the three types of nonroutine partnerships, in only one, new partners, is the need to know invested in the partnership. In the other two, the need to know is invested outside the partnership in various aspects of the job. In the mentor-learner partnership, mentors need to know how to "mold" the learners, while the learners need to know how to function within the organization. Because the partnership is viewed as temporary, the need to know for short-term partners concerns how to complete the tasks of the job. Only in a new partnership is the need to know recognized as the need to know how to partner. Paramedics in a new partnership attend to this need to know. Their experimentation as partners and with the partnership results in a confirmation of learning where knowing how to work together is tacit and actions are spontaneous. The nonroutine experience of being paired with another individual is no longer unusual. It has become routine.

Importance of Relationships to Workplace Learning

The importance of learning to partner can be visually demonstrated if one looks at routine and nonroutine partnerships in terms of the routine and nonroutine experiences of the job. Viewed in this manner, four combinations of partnership response to job experiences are possible, as displayed in Table 6.1.

Table 6.1. Responses to Job Experiences by Paramedic Partners

	Partnership	
Job Experiences	Routine	Nonroutine
Routine	Spontaneous	Tandem
Nonroutine	Synchronous	Individual

Responses by Routine Partners. The findings suggest that in the confirmation of learning to partner is the know-how to handle the routine and nonroutine job experiences within the context of the partnership. Paramedics in routine partnerships describe spontaneous performance in situations that both partners perceive as routine: "I would never have to ask him where he was in the procedure. I would just know." In nonroutine situations, they recognize the need to problem-solve, innovate and invent solutions, and test out those solutions until the problem is resolved. Their descriptions of these events contain the same themes. The pronoun "we" is used almost exclusively. The event is unusual, "a mess" as several paramedics suggest. The solution is accomplished in a series of "what ifs" followed by "what nexts." They learn to handle the situation as they proceed, but they work out the solution together. This learning process reflects Schön's (1983) reflection-in-action. The difference is that this process is engaged in by both partners in a synchronized fashion, whereas Schön describes professionals engaged in highly individualistic processes.

These responses to the nonroutine experiences of the job by paramedics in routine partnerships have their foundations in the partnership but are not encumbered by it. Because the partnership is a routine experience, it does not interfere with the demands of nonroutine job experiences. The process proposed for learning from experience holds that the longer the routine partnership persists, the more acquired experiences the partners will categorize as routine. This suggests that the routine partnership has the potential to be an increasingly effective working relationship as more job experiences are recognized as routine and handled spontaneously.

Responses by Nonroutine Partners. Paramedics engaged in the three nonroutine types of partnerships also face routine and nonroutine job experiences. As depicted in Table 6.1, their responses to these experiences differ from those of paramedics in routine partnerships. When the job experience is recognized as routine, the approach of the paramedics in all three types of nonroutine partnerships is to handle the situation in tandem, with one partner taking the lead and the other following that lead. Mentors say that they "make most of the patient care decisions." Short-term partners admit to saying, "It's my patient and it's your turn to drive." New partners report confusion. "You'll turn around to ask them to do something and they're gone."

When the job experience is nonroutine, the response is entirely different yet remains the same for all three types of nonroutine partnerships. Nonroutine partners respond to nonroutine experiences as individuals. When mentor-learner partners are faced with a nonroutine experience, the necessity of placing patient welfare over partner learning forces the mentor to step out of role and perform as an individual. The learner is an observer. Short-term partners reported feeling that these are situations where "I am by myself now," while new partners report doing everything twice.

Decision-making theory (Simon, 1965) suggests that the volume of information available to individuals from which decisions are made forces choices about what will be considered. When faced with two nonroutine experiences, the job and the partnership, each paramedic partner in a nonroutine partnership chose to ignore the partnership and attend to the job assignment.

Implications for the Practice of Continuing Professional Education

The experience of learning to work with another individual, like other informal learning experiences in this setting, can be explained by a process of experiential learning. It is within the descriptions of the phases of that process that the dynamics emerge and where adult educators might look for ways to enhance informal workplace learning. The influence on experiential learning of a perceived need to know and the necessity to experiment with new learning before it becomes explicit are open doors for innovative facilitation. Often the quality of learning achieved through informal learning strategies is of concern when this kind of learning is employed as a means of maintaining the competence of practicing professionals. If significant learning occurs through the employment of various informal learning strategies, then adaptation of these strategies into more formalized programs may provide not only an opportunity for new learning but also a mechanism whereby learning acquired through informal means may be reviewed, modified, or discarded as dysfunctional.

A fascination with content and skills, which seems to prevail in many continuing education programs, neglects the significant contributions to learning that can be made when professionals share informal learning experiences. Zemke (1990) points out that storytelling as a strategy for learning is often considered a less than legitimate workplace training technique. It is perhaps significant that even the name commonly applied to these tales of the workplace, "war stories," tends to cast them in a disparaging light. By demonstrating that shared experiences are significant in learning how to perform the job and how to function within the organization, storytelling is strengthened as a legitimate informal learning strategy, and one with significant potential in more formalized settings.

The discovery of the importance of partners in informal learning among paramedics was serendipitous. The definable events of their job assignments and the regularity of their workplace relationships provided a contextual backdrop against which the learning was distinguishable. The picture that emerges demonstrates the importance of the development of workplace relationships and the strategies employed for learning informally within the work environment. Together these offer points of focus for facilitation of informal and formal learning that enhances the workplace as a learning resource.

References

Argyris, C., and Schön, D. A. *Theory and Practice: Increasing Professional Effectiveness.* San Francisco: Jossey-Bass, 1974.

Carnevale, A., and Goldstein, H. *Employee Training and the National Standard.* Washington, D.C.: American Society for Training Development, 1983.

Jarvis, P. *Adult Learning in the Social Context.* London, England: Croom-Helm, 1987.

Kolb, D. A. *Experiential Learning: Experience as the Source of Learning and Development.* Englewood Cliffs, N.J.: Prentice Hall, 1984.

LaParo, M. E. "Health Care Middle Managers: What and How They Learn." Unpublished doctoral dissertation, Teachers College, Columbia University, 1989.

Marsick, V. J., and Watkins, K. E. "Approaches to Studying Learning in the Workplace." In V. J. Marsick (ed.), *Learning in the Workplace.* London, England: Croom-Helm, 1987.

Marsick, V. J., and Watkins, K. E. *Informal and Incidental Learning in the Workplace.* New York: Routledge & Kegan Paul, 1990.

Schön, D. A. *The Reflective Practitioner: How Professionals Think in Action.* New York: Basic Books, 1983.

Simon, H. A. *The Shape of Automation for Men and Management.* New York: HarperCollins, 1965.

Zemke, R. "Storytelling: Back to a Basic." *Training,* Mar. 1990, pp. 44–50.

BARBARA K. LOVIN, a paramedic, is associate professor in and chair of the Department of Health Sciences, School of Applied Sciences, Western Carolina University, Cullowhee, North Carolina.

Much of a professional's knowledge base is implicit. This way of knowing plays a distinctive role in medical problem solving, yet education has been slow to acknowledge its validity.

Harnessing Implicit Knowing to Improve Medical Practice

Nicholas C. Boreham

Everyday experience suggests that professional people possess and act on knowledge that they cannot bring to consciousness or express verbally. As an educator, I once followed a consultant physician on his hospital ward round. He reviewed a patient's treatment and prescribed drug A. A junior physician asked him why he had prescribed that particular drug, because in such cases it was usual to prescribe drug B. The consultant said, "Well, B's a bit . . . ," and here he made a gesture with two hands that I can imitate but not describe. He was unable to explain the matter further, but his response seemed to satisfy the junior, and the ward round continued.

Afterward, I asked the junior physician why such an articulate person as the consultant had been unable to explain how the pharmacological properties of drug B ruled it out for that patient. He replied that the consultant's behavior was not at all uncommon. Not only was this eminent and articulate specialist frequently unable to explain *why* he had taken a particular course of action, he was sometimes *unaware of the actual course of action that he had taken.* This story draws attention to an assumption that often underlies discussions of both medical education and practice, namely, that the knowledge base of a profession can be made *explicit.* Knowledge is explicit when the practitioner is aware of it and can express it verbally.

In medical education, the content of both the preclinical course and the clinical course are treated as bodies of explicit knowledge. This assumption is obvious in the system of licensing examinations, which poses questions to be answered orally or in writing. Explicitness is assumed in medical practice when problem solving is represented as a conscious process of focusing attention on signs and symptoms, possible

NEW DIRECTIONS FOR ADULT AND CONTINUING EDUCATION, no. 55, Fall 1992 © Jossey-Bass Publishers

diagnoses, data obtained from investigations, and so on, with all the key interpretations and decisions placed unambiguously in the medical record.

However, as the above incident suggests, it is important to recognize that there is also an *implicit* way of knowing. Implicit knowing occurs when one remains unaware of precisely *what* he or she knows and cannot put it into words.

The first scientific studies of implicit knowing date only from the nineteenth century. There were a handful of investigations of patients suffering from amnesia carried out by their own physicians. These physicians reported cases who had suffered memory loss through physical or psychological trauma, in the sense of not being able to consciously recall previous experiences, but who otherwise acted as if they were fully cognizant of these events. For example, Schacter (1987) quotes the account by the English surgeon Dunn (1845) of a woman rescued from drowning. After her recovery from a long coma, she was unable to remember things that happened to her but nonetheless learned dressmaking. She did this without being able to consciously recall what she had been taught. Her ability to remember explicitly had been destroyed, yet she could still acquire knowledge, store it, and use it. Schacter sees this as one of the earliest pieces of evidence that there is an implicit way of knowing that can operate independently of the explicit.

Such findings made little impression on mainstream psychology. The assumption remained what it had been for most of Western cultural history: If we cannot state something, then we do not know it. The refusal to acknowledge the existence of implicit memory might have been due to the often outrageous claims about the influence of the unconscious on human behavior made by psychoanalysts in the early part of the century. Today, however, implicit knowing has become a serious subject for research. The implications for professional practice in medicine, as for all of the knowledge-based professions, are considerable.

In this chapter, I review the evidence for the implicit-explicit distinction, distinguish among three different ways in which professional knowledge can be implicit, and discuss the contribution of implicit ways of knowing to medical problem solving. At the same time, questions are raised about the implications for continuing professional education.

Three Kinds of Implicitness

So far, I have used the word *implicit* to refer to knowledge that is both impossible to verbalize and inaccessible to consciousness. This is the kind of implicitness that has been studied by experimental psychologists such as Reber and Broadbent. However, in the messier world of professional practice, it appears that there are several different kinds of implicitness. Here, I draw attention to just three. In addition to knowledge that is both impossible to verbalize and unavailable to consciousness, other knowledge is impossible to verbalize but *is* available to consciousness, and still other knowledge is both verbalizable and available to consciousness but is not made explicit in the usual course of professional practice.

Unconscious and Nonverbalizable Knowing: Familiarity with the Structure of a Stimulus Environment. The basis for the implicit learning of languages, claims Reber, is the human capacity identified by Hasher and Zacks (1984) for automatically recording the frequency and covariation of stimuli in the environment. In addition to storing conscious perceptions of things that catch our attention, to which we assign verbalizable meaning (for instance, "What a strange hat!"), Hasher and Zacks have demonstrated that we also automatically store environmental stimulus patterns. This unconscious data base guides our conscious perceptions. As Reber (1989, p. 230) states, "The proper stance is to assume that unconscious mental processes are the foundations upon which emerging conscious operations are laid." In other words, when we enter a familiar environment, unconscious processes trigger expectations that structure the explicit mental activity that we experience as conscious, verbal reasoning.

Many professional medical judgments appear to be shaped by unconscious perception of this kind. The importance of implicit knowing is stressed in an influential textbook on general medical practice by Roger Neighbour, who says that one of the main criteria for telling a good consultation from a bad one is "the doctor's ability to pay attention to clues and events in the periphery of his vision" (1987, p. 7). Much the same point is made by Hull (1985, p. 14), another physician, who refers to "that useful warning light, which all of us recognise, that suddenly lights up to announce that there is something unusual." He gives the following example: "One summer a farmer patient of mine started selling off his prize friesian herd and I noticed that he started putting his best grazing land under the plow. While I was speculating what he was up to, I was called to see his herdsman, an uncomplaining Italian, who had 'flu, and so instantly I diagnosed my first case of Brucellosis, because the various observed facts suddenly formed a pattern" (p. 14).

This example carries the hallmarks of implicit memory. The provisional diagnosis was not made by deliberately focusing conscious attention on abnormal signs and symptoms, then eliminating alternative disease hypotheses by explicit reasoning processes. It appears to have been formed automatically at an unconscious level where it activated the word *Brucellosis* in Hull's explicit memory store before he became conscious of what was happening. Just as significant is Hull's account of how he acquired this ability—by familiarizing himself with his work environment. When he took up his practice, he tells us, he read the complete medical record of every patient on his list and acquainted himself, as far as possible, with the locality in which the practice was situated. Arguably, in this way he acquired an unconscious domain map of the kind discussed by Hasher and Zacks (1984). Presented with the symptoms of influenza at the wrong time of year, Hull unconsciously integrated these data into a significant pattern at the level of implicit memory. This triggered his explicit knowledge of medicine and delivered the name of the disease into his consciousness.

To develop this kind of implicit knowing, it is necessary to obtain extensive familiarity with the problem domain. However, the acquisition of an implicit knowledge base requires more than access to the data; it also calls for the opportunity to engage in *unselective learning*. Unselective learning entails openness to the complex interplay of variables in the environment (Hayes and Broadbent, 1988). It contrasts with *selective learning*, the process of focusing attention on key variables followed by verbalization of what has been learned. The importance of unselective learning is clear from the work of Reber (1989), who shows that the actions of consciously searching for solution rules and verbalizing them tend to suppress the natural process of acquiring an implicit knowledge base. The need to reduce training time, and a natural bias toward didacticism, impels many instructors to prefer selective learning. It is difficult for them to appreciate that immersing somebody in a task environment without requiring focused attention and formulation of explicit "how-to" rules can be beneficial.

Conscious but Nonverbalizable Knowing: Feeling-Sense. All professionals develop a "feel" for practice situations. This is another kind of implicit knowing, distinct from the first kind in that the professional may be aware of the feeling-sense but unable to verbalize it. Some psychologists view the feeling component of problem solving as a by-product of purely cognitive processing. However, I prefer Jung's ([1921] 1971, pp. 434–435) view that feeling is a separate function that plays a distinctive part in decision making: "Feeling is a kind of judgment, differing from intellectual judgment in that its aim is not to establish conceptual relations but to set up a subjective criterion of acceptance or rejection."

While few patients would be happy if their doctors relied solely on this way of assessing their needs, the feeling function undoubtedly makes a valuable contribution to medical problem solving. For example, among the most difficult cases requiring skilled investigation in the hospital emergency room is the febrile child. The high temperature might be nothing serious, or it might be caused by a life-threatening infection.

Crain and Crain (1987) compared expert physicians with less experienced ones at work in the emergency room. They found that the former followed a different strategy for assessing the febrile child—obtaining a general impression of the patient before attempting an explicit diagnosis. Unlike their less experienced colleagues, they interacted with the child in warm and friendly ways and thus obtained a feeling-sense of the problem before they were able to *say* what the problem was. Crain and Crain interpreted this feeling-sense as a way of knowing that is quite different from conceptual knowing. It was only through it that the expert physicians were able to differentiate children who were seriously ill from those whose high temperatures were of no significance. Obviously, they had learned something from their previous experience, presumably the "feel" of a child who is dangerously ill. They were able to activate this knowledge by interacting with their patients, but they could not put the knowledge into words. They certainly did not learn it out of a textbook.

Acquisition of this kind of implicit knowing calls for a curriculum that encourages acceptance of the premise that there are valid ways of knowing other than the intellectual. Actually, this is asking a lot, for throughout history, Western academic culture has tended to regard emotion as a source of bias in serious science, and the higher education curriculum has downgraded it accordingly. I am not arguing for the subversion of rational thought by feeling. Rather, it should act as a subsidiary function, augmenting explicit knowing. Continuing professional education can encourage this by mentoring that promotes learning in the workplace in a manner receptive to the learner's feeling-sense.

Unstated Conscious and Verbalizable Knowing: Hidden Assumptions of Professional Practice. Knowledge can also be implicit not because it is stored in a memory system that is inaccessible to consciousness or because it is an ineffable feeling-sense, but because it is outside the current focus of our attention.

According to Polyani (1958), most of the knowledge that influences our supposedly "scientific" thinking is implicit in this way. He distinguishes between focal thinking (when we focus our attention on something) and tacit thinking (the vast range of our past life experiences that are not the focus of current attention but that color our interpretation of what is in focus). In Polanyi's view, our understanding of the object of attention is a projection of our hidden assumptions. Thus, all seemingly objective knowing is biased to some extent by our own individual standpoints. This is a different kind of implicitness from that defined by Reber and Broadbent, because much of this knowledge is in principle both verbalizable and open to awareness. However, most of the time we make little attempt to bring it into focus.

People have good reasons for keeping things out of focus. Explicit mention of something that we find threatening is almost the same as experiencing it. This may be why in family therapy, as DiNicola (1988) points out, much of the interaction does not operate at the level of the explicit meaning of the words or of the behavior that occurs but rather at the level of what is implicitly meant by these occurrences. Such messages "do not have to be understood or grasped on a conscious level to work" (1988, p. 5).

The practice of keeping things out of focus can have a sinister purpose. Those responsible for deciding priorities for health care may protect themselves by keeping their assumptions out of the public arena. As Hilfiker (1983, p. 717) comments, "The old, chronically ill, debilitated, or mentally impaired do not receive the same level of aggressive medical evaluation and treatment as the young, acutely ill, and mentally normal. *We do not discuss this reality or debate its ethics*" (emphasis added).

Promotion of the third kind of implicit knowing is a matter of opening professional practice to debate. Newcomers to a profession are often critical of the practices that it hides from the public, but they can be rapidly socialized into accepting them. To ensure renewal, leaders of professions must adopt the attitude expressed in the maxim, "Don't try to be as good as me; you must try to be *better* than me."

Contributions of Implicit Knowing to Medical Problem Solving

But what specifically can implicit knowing contribute to medical practice? There are at least two aspects of medical problem solving that appear to be facilitated by implicit knowing: coping with complexity and communicating with the patient.

Coping with Complexity. In the research by Broadbent (1989), not all tasks were facilitated by the acquisition of an implicit knowledge base. The kind that it did facilitate tended to be complex tasks in which the solutions could be attained only by understanding the interrelationships among numerous interacting variables. A possible explanation is that the capacity limitations of short-term memory prevent learners from representing complex problems explicitly, but they can be understood at an implicit level because implicit memory has no effective limitations.

The problem facing many physicians is that "anything can walk through the door." There are many thousands of diseases in the International Classification of Disease, most with numerous manifestations. Yet, the average physician has insufficient time or resources for an explicit investigation of every possibility. As the research by Elstein, Shulman, and Sprafka (1978) showed, what distinguishes the expert physician is not superiority at investigating disease hypotheses but rather the ability to select the most likely hypothesis to begin with. A possible explanation of this ability is that the expert selects his or her hypotheses by the unconscious perception of the complex of factors that have led a particular patient to report a particular symptom at a particular moment in time. It is likely that the objective patient data are colored by a perception of implicit patterns in the patient's medical history, the medical history of his or her family, and the pattern of morbidity in the community, together with a feeling for the significance of the patient's attitude, recent life events, and so on. In short, the way in which the expert practitioner copes with complexity could well be by unconsciously registering enough situational constraints to automatically focus conscious attention on the most promising provisional diagnosis.

Communicating with the Patient. Central to medical practice is the consultation. Successful communication between physician and patient in this encounter depends on each side being explicit with the other about certain crucial matters. However, it also depends on the expectations that each participant has of the other, and these often remain irredeemably implicit.

An example of the implicitness of physician-patient expectations is provided by the Balint seminars, a series of case conferences for general practitioners organized by the London psychiatrist Michael Balint. Among the cases discussed was the pseudonymous Miss Malvern, a puzzling patient who was nonetheless treated very successfully by her physician. Her case was discussed in the Balint seminars for two years before it was realized that the breakthrough in the physician's understanding of the problem had occurred in a moment in which the patient expressed anger: "Only much later, in fact not until two years later, did we comprehend that this brief emotional interchange, which at the time of reporting [to the seminar] seemed casual, introductory and anecdotal, was really of great importance. . . . The reporting doctor had in fact used the emotional content of the interview for his overall diagnosis and treatment plan without at the time having been fully aware of its importance. Obviously the doctor had at that time perceived something in the patient which had struck a chord in him, and he was able to convey this understanding to her" (Clyne, 1973, p. 74).

Conclusion

The evidence discussed in this chapter suggests that implicit knowing makes its main contribution at the initial stages of medical problem solving, establishing effective communication with the patient and achieving early insight into his or her problem. This is the stage of the consultation that Neighbour (1987) describes as "connecting." If it is done successfully, the problem becomes amenable to representation in the explicit terms that are taught in medical school. This is because the number of practicable lines of action will by then have shrunk to a manageable list that permits conscious comparison among alternatives. It is also because, as the physician's investigation proceeds, it begins to generate objective data for which there are explicit techniques of analysis. The explicit way of knowing stressed in medical education and practice has enormous power to solve medical problems. But we do not always recognize that it may require an implicit way of knowing to bring it to bear.

Although the practical implications of implicit knowing that are addressed here derive from the medical field, they reach well beyond medicine. Any profession in which needed knowledge is highly complex and contextual, and in which there are interactive components between the professional and the client, can find the conclusions drawn to be equally applicable.

References

Broadbent, D.,E. "Effective Decisions and Their Verbal Justification." *Philosophical Transactions of the Royal Society of London,* 1989, *B327,* 493–502.

Clyne, M. B. "The Diagnosis." In E. Balint and J. S. Norrell (eds.), *Six Minutes for the Patient.* London, England: Tavistock/Routledge & Kegan Paul, 1973.

Crain, W. C., and Crain, E. F. "The Psychology of the Scientist: Can Humanistic Theory Contribute to Our Understanding of Medical Problem Solving?" *Psychological Reports,* 1987, *61,* 779–788.

DiNicola, V. S. "Saying It and Meaning It: Forging an Ethic for Family Therapy." *Journal of Strategic and Systematic Therapies,* 1988, *7,* 1–7.

Dunn, R. "Case of Suspension of the Mental Faculties." *Lancet,* 1845, *2,* 588–590.

Elstein, A. S., Shulman, L. S., and Sprafka, S. A. *Medical Problem Solving.* Cambridge, Mass.: Harvard University Press, 1978.

Hasher, L., and Zacks, R. T. "Automatic Processing of Fundamental Information." *American Psychologist,* 1984, *39,* 1372–1388.

Hayes, N. A., and Broadbent, D. E. "Two Modes of Learning for Interactive Tasks." *Cognition,* 1988, *28,* 249–276.

Hilfiker, F. "Allowing the Debilitated to Die." *New England Journal of Medicine,* 1983, *308,* 716–719.

Hull, F. M. "The Consultation Process." In M. Sheldon, J. Brooke, and A. Rector (eds.), *Decision Making in General Practice.* London, England: Macmillan, 1985.

Jung, C. G. *Psychological Types.* London: Routledge & Kegan Paul, 1971. (Originally published 1921.)

Neighbour, R. *The Inner Consultation.* Lancaster, England: MTP Press, 1987.

Polyani, M. *Personal Knowledge: Toward a Post-Critical Philosophy.* Chicago: University of Chicago Press, 1958.

Reber, A. S. "Implicit Learning and Tacit Knowledge." *Journal of Experimental Psychology: General,* 1989, *118,* 219–235.

Schacter, D. L. "Implicit Memory: History and Current Status." *Journal of Experimental Psychology: Learning, Memory, and Cognition,* 1987, *13,* 501–518.

NICHOLAS C. BOREHAM *is director of the Center for Adult and Higher Education, School of Education, University of Manchester, England.*

Awareness of women's learning models lends insight that enriches an understanding of both women's and men's learning.

Models of Women's Learning: Implications for Continuing Professional Education

Kathleen A. Loughlin, Vivian Wilson Mott

Recent feminist research—for instance, the works of Gilligan (1982), Jordan and others (1991), and Belenky, Clinchy, Goldberger, and Tarule (1986)—suggests that there may be a difference in the ways that women and men know and learn. The themes of women's "relatedness" and "connectedness" in relation to meaning making surface as the primary characteristics that may differentiate women's knowing from men's knowing. Furthermore, this research, in providing descriptive qualifiers such as relatedness and connectedness, sets the foundation for emerging models of women's learning.

Caution, however, is needed when interpreting these insights from feminist research. Formulation of models of women's learning may create a divisive polarity: women know and learn one way, men another. Characteristics of knowing and learning may then be rigidly interpreted as gender-based, closing off the possibility for mutual enrichment in understanding the processes of knowing and learning. An alternative interpretation, however, is also possible. Formulation of these models also creates an opportunity to transcend this polarity and ask, What insights can be gleaned from these models that can be applied to enrich both women's and men's learning in their continuing professional education? The discussion in this chapter is in response to that question. Through continuing exploration, therefore, the contribution that an awareness of women's learning models can make to continuing professional education is developed. The chapter includes a brief overview of two studies related to women's learning models, a discussion of selected findings from these studies, and an identification of implications for continuing professional education practice.

Two Studies Related to Women's Learning Models

Women's learning, as based on critical reflection on underlying assumptions of knowledge and newly constructed understandings, was central to the qualitative studies conducted by Hart, Karlovic, Loughlin, and Meyer (1991) and Mott (1991). Twenty-four women participated in the first study, each of whom acted as a social change agent on behalf of women's rights. Their social action was primarily through the media, education, or politics. The study's purpose was to gain insight into the learning experiences that facilitated their ability to make commitments, to take risks, and to act creatively for change within society. These women were middle-class Caucasians, ranging in age from the late twenties to early seventies. To collect data, semistructured interviews were used. The data were then analyzed using a modified form of the constant comparative method.

The study by Mott included eight women who had achieved success within traditionally male-dominated professions, such as engineering, manufacturing, and the military. These women had initially been part of an earlier study by Mott that sought to elaborate on the career and educational implications of the model of knowing developed by Belenky, Clinchy, Goldberger, and Tarule (1986). The purpose of Mott's second study, though, was to discover and critique the underlying assumptions of these professional women's way of knowing. Through critical reflection on these assumptions, the women sought to identify the influence that these assumptions had on their values, meaning construction, and decision making. The sample consisted of seven Caucasian women and one African American woman. They ranged in age from the early thirties to mid-fifties. During group meetings, which focused on topics such as career challenges and political and social responsibilities, data were collected. The data analysis was guided by a comparative analysis method.

While these two qualitative studies were designed for different purposes, common themes emerged in the findings of the studies. Central to this commonality is the emergence of insights into women's learning models.

To introduce the findings of both studies, we begin with an overview of the nature of the learning that these women experienced in relation to models of women's learning. The discussion continues with an exploration of three specific findings from the studies that contribute insight into models of women's learning.

The Nature of Learning in the Two Studies in Relation to Models of Women's Learning. All of the women in the two studies were involved in learning that was not confined to particular contexts. Rather, the learning achieved through self-reflection on their daily concrete life experiences influenced both their personal and professional development. The nature of that learning was grounded in critical reflection on the underlying assumptions of their personal and professional knowledge. The insights that they then gleaned motivated their action, sometimes within their personal lives and other times within their professional lives. Mott succinctly characterizes the effects of this learning for the women in both studies. These women became more able to integrate their personal and professional identities. They also became more self-directed in the choices that they made, and their ability to tolerate ambiguity increased.

While the nature of this learning had a significant influence in these women's lives, the process that they experienced—a praxis of critical reflection and action—does not suggest characteristics that would classify it as a model of women's learning. To identify the commonality between their learning and such a model, then, it is necessary to examine the underlying relationship between the knower and the known. An analysis of this relationship is at the heart of models of women's knowing and learning.

For example, Belenky, Clinchy, Goldberger, and Tarule (1986) identify five different perspectives or descriptions of the relationship between the knower and the known. The first two perspectives of silence and received knowing reflect a woman's loss of self and her complete dependence on authority for knowledge. Subjective knowing, the third perspective, is founded on a woman's trust in intuitive knowing as the source of her knowledge. The fourth perspective, procedural knowing, consists of two different approaches to meaning making. In each, a woman has a sense of herself as knower in relation to the known. For a separate knower, her procedures of knowing are objective in relation to the known and are based on logic. On the other hand, for a connected knower, her procedures of knowing involve building a connection to the known and are based on empathy. The final perspective, constructed knowing, represents a woman's integration of reason and intuition in constructing her knowledge. Belenky, Clinchy, Goldberger, and Tarule's identification of the underlying direction of movement among the perspectives—knowing that moves toward connectedness and integration of reason and intuition—is an example of the central characteristic that defines women's models of knowing and learning.

The insights from the studies outlined earlier also reflect this movement toward women's integration of reason and intuition in their knowing. The following discussion of three specific findings from these studies, therefore, is within the framework of models of women's knowing and learning. The first finding suggests that learning that involves critical reflection and action includes a knowing centered in authenticity. The second finding implies that this learning leads to the construction of knowledge that motivates action. The third finding suggests that this type of learning is a relational process within the context of the concrete experiences of daily living.

Learning That Involves Critical Reflection and Action Includes a Knowing Centered in Authenticity. As the women who were social change agents reflected on the learning experiences that had influenced their willingness to make commitments, to take risks, and to act creatively for change within society, a common theme emerged. They each spoke of an awareness of their personal uniqueness and of a fidelity to that uniqueness within that learning. This sense of authenticity in their learning seemed to be manifested in their ability to be self-defined and to trust the creative interaction of their unique genetic endowments and their life events. Cell (1984, p. 20) describes this process as one of "deriving our beliefs from our own experience." In being true to their personal uniqueness, these change agents' self-determination involved trusting their own experiences and listening to the voices of their authentic selves in their knowing.

For each of these women, the voice of her authentic self emerged in her experience of intuitive promptings within her knowing. In listening to the voice of her authentic self and in centering her knowing in that self, each woman experienced a sense authorship of the knowledge that she constructed. This intuitive sense, however, was not the sole source of their knowing. Rather, their knowing involved an integration of these intuitive promptings with reason—the constructed knowing perspective (Belenky, Clinchy, Goldberger, and Tarule, 1986). Succinctly, these change agents' centering of their knowing in their authentic selves appeared to be a characteristic of a learning process based on critical reflection and action.

For example, the presence of the authentic self in knowing was expressed by Joyce, a participant in Hart, Karlovic, Loughlin, and Meyer's study of social change agents. A commissioner of parole within a state penal system, Joyce recalled her early awareness of the influence of this authentic self in her knowing. As a young adult in a Jewish family, she had attended Saturday school in an affluent Jewish neighborhood. She described her reaction of railing against the religious beliefs taught at Saturday school. As Joyce reflected, "I confused the religious beliefs with the value systems, which of course is all wrong. And I knew it at the time, but I just knew I didn't fit in." She explained her subsequent actions: "So consequently I didn't pursue a life of being a traditional housewife, joining a country club, and living in a style to which I was groomed."

Joyce described this experience of her authentic self with the words "but I just knew I didn't fit in." Her experience of owning that voice and integrating it with the voice of reason guided her subsequent actions.

Similarly, Susan, an educator, also spoke of experiencing the presence of her authentic self when she decided to pursue a doctoral program. Her intellectual interests included ethics, psychology, and sociology. Most doctoral programs, however, were defined by disciplines. She described her conflict at the time since what she "was involved in seemed to fall between the cracks of the various disciplines." Rather than abandon her interests, she "looked and found an opportunity to design an inter-disciplinary program that was independent learning." She reflected, "This was very important because I knew it fit."

The onset of awareness of this intuitive sense of knowing—Joyce's "I just knew" and Susan's "I knew it fit"—seems to be the beginning of owning authentic knowing. Although other women in the study used different words to describe this experience, such as "a growing sense" and "an inner sense within me," the influence of the authentic self in knowing emerged in each woman's reflection.

In essence, the learning of these social change agents, which involved critical reflection and action, seemed to include an enduring trust and ownership of the authentic self as the center of their knowing. The importance of owning the presence of the authentic self, as suggested in the lives of these change agents, is that this ownership creates the opportunity for a woman to acknowledge the value of intuition in her knowing.

This valuing of intuition was also a prominent theme in the reflections of the eight women in Mott's study who were working in traditionally male-dominated professions. It appears that when a woman owns her intuitive knowing, she has the opportunity to integrate the knowledge of reason with the knowledge of intuition. For these women, this knowing became the basis for learning that involves critical reflection and action.

Learning That Includes Critical Reflection Based on Authentic Knowing Leads to the Construction of Knowledge That Motivates Action. These women's critical reflection on the underlying assumptions of their personal and professional knowledge initiated a learning process that allowed them to see their worlds from a different perspective. For instance, Miriam, a political scientist, commented on her critical reflection on the underlying assumptions of the knowledge that framed her personal experience. She began graduate school when her children were young, and day care was a necessity to help her manage all of her personal and family responsibilities. Although she was accepted into prestigious universities, the demands at home created conflict for her, which she translated into a sense of guilt. At that time, however, Miriam began to speak with other women and found that they too felt conflict and guilt. As they spoke, Miriam was able to move away from feelings of "being the only one with a problem." She began to realize "that these conflicts we shared, that they were deep and they weren't easily solved." In looking at the reasons for these problems and the underlying assumptions of those reasons, she developed an alternative understanding of her dilemma. While the demands on her time continued, her critique and authentic knowing of the inequities within society led her to develop a vision of society that attended to the needs of "the dispossessed." This vision motivated her to commit herself to scholarly research on behalf of those persons not valued in society. The reflections of Miriam and the other women in this study on change agents also suggest that their learning process included critical reflection, authentic knowing, and the creation of a vision that inspired them to act.

Another illustration of this learning process was Louise's experience of becoming motivated to seek public office. A lawyer, Louise's learning began with her authentic knowing of her experiences as a district attorney. In this capacity, she met with battered women who were covered with bruises and had no place to go. The law responded to these women by issuing protective court orders stating that their husbands would be in contempt of court at the next battering. Louise's empathic knowing of these experiences of meeting these women caused her to critique the underlying assumptions of the laws designed to protect the rights and well-being of victims. This critique then led her to envision a society governed by laws that effectively protected its citizens. She described her realization that as district attorney she was "dealing with the results of policies. And my feeling was that somehow if the only way that you could change these policies was to do this, then you run for office." Her motivation for action was that she "wanted to run to make a difference." The difference she sought to make—the passage of new laws—was motivated by a learning process that included critical reflection and authentic knowing.

Action that emanates from critical reflection and authentic knowing also includes personal and professional development. The action that the women in traditionally male-dominated professions were engaged in focused on personal growth that enriched their professional commitments. These women spoke of becoming more confident and assertive in both their personal and professional lives. From their reflection on the underlying assumptions of their knowledge, they changed to feel freer to express their personal expectations within their professions. Additionally, these women were able to take advantage of opportunities in their lives by becoming more flexible.

From these studies, insight into the relationship between learning, knowing, and acting emerged. Learning that leads to action, these studies suggest, involves critical reflection, authentic knowing, and the creation of new knowledge and visions that then inspire action.

Learning That Involves Critical Reflection, Authentic Knowing, and Action Is a Relational Process Within the Context of the Concrete Experiences of Daily Living. Although formal education is part of the concrete experiences of daily life, these women's formal educational experiences did not appear to facilitate this type of learning process. Rather, some women found these formal educational experiences alienating. For example, Edith, a cofounder of an international educational center, described her reaction about returning to formal education. She judged that "a whole side of ways of knowing are not generally addressed in the academy. . . . You feel that whole parts of you are left out most times when I'm back at school." She characterized her experience as "spiritually starving because I have to leave out whole parts of me in the process which are very important to me."

The eight women in the traditionally male-dominated professions also critiqued their formal educational experiences. They assessed that at times formal education failed to meet and support their needs as learners. In response, they engaged in self-directed learning. This learning, while self-directed, was not experienced in isolation but rather in a context of relatedness. A specific example in these professional women's lives was the learning and critical reflection that occurred within their weekly meetings together. A bond of connective interacting had developed among them that enabled them to meet their unique learning needs.

Chodorow (1987) has used the word *relatedness* to describe this bond because it emphasizes a woman's underlying psychic presence to others. This presence forms the basis for a connective interaction with others. A context of relatedness appears to create the opportunity for women to connect their critical reflection and authentic knowing with the experiences of others and public and professional issues. This experience of psychic relatedness may occur within a group of women who are physically present to one another, as was characteristic of the meetings of the eight women in Mott's study.

An experience of this relatedness emerged as both a catalyst and a context for the learning process within the lives of the women in both studies. Additionally, this learning process occurred most often in the diverse experiences of daily life. The underlying commonality of these experiences was the connective interaction and the sense of relatedness.

Implications for Continuing Professional Education Practice

This chapter was developed in response to the question, What insights can be gleaned from models of women's learning that can be applied to enrich both women's and men's learning in their continuing professional education? The underlying assumption of that question is that insight into the nature of the learning process can transcend gender polarities and be appreciated as a starting point for a richer understanding of learning for both women and men. A second issue, however, emerges when attempts are made to address the implications of the two studies reviewed. This issue is that the research focused on a specific learning process: critical reflection and action based on newly constructed understandings. Does this type of learning have relevance to continuing professional education?

An affirmative response might be given by professional educators who not only attend to the content to be learned but also view the learning process as empowering. For professional educators who seek to facilitate learners' development of integrated professional identities, their ability to tolerate ambiguity, and their capacity to make commitments and take responsible risks, insight into the specific learning process of critical reflection and action is advantageous.

While individual educators might see other implications from these studies and from women's learning models, three specific implications are of interest here: Professional educators are called upon (1) to facilitate a process of centering learners' knowing within their authentic self, (2) to facilitate the development of a connected and experientially focused language within the learning process, and (3) to create a context of relatedness among learners. Since these three implications are interrelated, the following brief description of a possible continuing education program is presented to clarify each.

This program would begin with an orientation experience for learners that facilitates their development of an awareness of different ways of knowing in a professional context and the advantages of each. The educator might also use this orientation session to gather data on the learning styles of the individuals involved. Since authenticity suggests fidelity to an individual's uniqueness, continuing professional education programs could be individualized in order to accommodate diverse learning styles.

The central focus of this orientation would be on the process of centering learners' knowing in their authentic selves. This process would involve three cyclical actions: learners' commitment making, action, and reflection, all within a significant professional experience. The professional experiences to which learners choose to commit themselves as the starting points of their continuing professional education programs would differ. Also, the opportunity to freely choose the ways to meet the demands of those particular professional experiences would also be important.

As learners worked through these professional experiences, they would commit themselves to reflect on their processes of knowing and the influence of that knowing on the resolution of their particular professional tasks. Journal writing and small group discussions on their thoughts and experiences would help create insights. The language used to reflect on these different ways of knowing would necessarily involve words and concepts drawn from their experiences and would also connect to the emotional and physical components in their knowing.

At mutually agreeable times, the educator and learners would meet for collective reflection on their processes of knowing within the professional setting. A responsibility of the educator would be to facilitate the creation of an affective and psychic bond among group members: a context of relatedness. Learners would be encouraged to share specific parts of their knowing—the rational and the intuitive. Through group reflection, models of different ways of knowing that significantly and positively influence professional practice would be identified and validated.

Building on these models, the educator would encourage learners to use reflection to develop a model of their unique professional way of knowing, one centered on their authentic selves. This model would then become the basis for developing a continuing professional education program that meets the needs of both the professional and the organization. Within this program, learners would again commit themselves to the same process of reflection and action in professional experiences. However, this time and in the times that follow, the learners' choices would involve identification of professional experiences that were problematic and caused uncertainty for them. Their need for content would emerge within the context of working through those experiences. The educator, then, assumes the role of resource for content, while maintaining the roles of nurturer and challenger within the learning process.

Conclusion

Briefly described, this continuing professional education program is grounded in a context of relatedness. Similar to the learning process of the women in the two studies described here, the learning process suggested for professionals includes critical reflection, authentic knowing, and action on experience. This vision of the learning process hints at the creative challenges that face continuing professional educators today. In professional worlds marked by uncertainty and continuous change, these challenges call upon continuing professional educators, women and men, to facilitate education that leads professionals to make commitments, to take risks, and to act creatively and responsibly within their professional organizations.

References

Belenky, M. F., Clinchy, B. M., Goldberger, N. R., and Tarule, J. M. *Women's Ways of Knowing: The Development of Self, Voice, and Mind.* New York: Basic Books, 1986.

Cell, E. *Learning to Learn from Experience.* Albany: State University of New York Press, 1984.

Chodorow, N. "Feminism and Difference: Gender, Relation, and Differences in Psychoanalytic Perspective." In M. R. Walsh (ed.), *The Psychology of Women: Ongoing Debates.* New Haven, Conn.: Yale University Press, 1987.

Gilligan, C. *In a Different Voice: Psychological Theory and Women's Development.* Cambridge, Mass.: Harvard University Press, 1982.

Hart, M., Karlovic, N., Loughlin, K. A., and Meyer, S. "Reconstructing the Adult Education Enterprise: The Value of Feminist Theory for Adult Education." In M. Langenbach (ed.), *Proceedings of the 32nd Annual Adult Education Research Conference.* Norman: University of Oklahoma, 1991.

Jordan, J. V., and others. *Women's Growth in Connection: Writings from the Stone Center.* New York: Guilford, 1991.

Mott, V. W. "Women's Ways of Knowing: Effects of Success in a Man's World." In *Professionals' Ways of Knowing and the Implications for CPE.* Preconference Proceedings of the Commission for Continuing Professional Education, American Association for Adult and Continuing Education. Montreal, Quebec, Canada: Commission for Continuing Professional Education, American Association for Adult and Continuing Education, 1991. (ED 339 848)

KATHLEEN A. LOUGHLIN *is associate professor of adult education at Saint Joseph's College, Brooklyn, New York. She is also a visiting assistant professor of adult education at Teachers College, Columbia University, New York City.*

VIVIAN WILSON MOTT *is a doctoral student in adult education at the University of Georgia, Athens. She is also owner of Wilson Mott & Associates, a training design and management firm.*

Practical knowledge has returned to a place of respectability in recent literature on professional learning, and it is once again acknowledged as an important component of professional practice.

Learning Practical Knowledge

Peter Jarvis

> What I hear, I cannot remember
> What I see, I do remember
> What I do, I understand
> —Chinese Proverb

The Chinese proverb above well summarizes the teaching and learning of practical knowledge. In this chapter, I explore issues pertaining to practical knowledge, especially from the perspective of learning. First, I argue that there are three dimensions to practical knowledge; next, I examine how we learn it; finally, I briefly consider its relationship to skill.

Practical Knowledge

Ryle raised the question of practical knowledge in a seminal study in 1949. He distinguished between *knowledge how* and *knowledge that* and suggested that in everyday life "we are more concerned with people's competencies than with their cognitive repertoires" (Ryle, 1963, p. 28). Here he was attacking the intellectual emphasis on theoretical knowledge, and yet he oversimplified the problem by adopting a behaviorist solution, suggesting that when "I am doing something intelligently . . . I am doing one thing and not two" (p. 32). But "knowing how" and "being able" are not synonymous! Scheffler (1965) also recognizes this distinction, noting that a person might know how to drive a car but be prevented from doing so for a variety of reasons, such as having a broken leg. There are contingencies that cannot always be controlled. Hence, the difference between having the knowledge and being able to perform the action still remains crucial. However, this illustration does not probe deeply enough, for there is another salient question: When people say "I know how to . . . ," does their use of the phrase "know how" have any cognitive orientation at all? They might actually be using the phrase incorrectly! For instance, it might actually be more correct to claim that "I am able to . . . ," rather than "I know how to. . . ." In other words, the possession of a skill does not necessarily always mean that people have all of the knowledge how, although there may well be other occasions when they actually have or have had that knowledge.

Knowing how is not the whole story. When experts perform an action, they do so knowing that there is a likely outcome. It is *knowing that* there is a likely outcome that constitutes another element in practical knowledge. Not only do experts know, but those who observe expert behavior know what the outcome of a skill or occupational performance is likely to be. For instance, car drivers know that when the car is moving, if they depress the brake, the car is most likely to slow down. Experts do not only know how, but they know that something will most likely happen when they apply that know-how. Now, it could be claimed that this is theoretical knowledge, and in one sense it is. However, it is suggested here that this type of knowledge is *knowing that,* and that this is a form of practical knowledge because it is about what happens in practice. It is knowledge gained by practicing or observing practice. This is the knowledge of practice. If it is theoretical, as I have suggested elsewhere (Jarvis, 1991), then it is only theoretical insofar as it reports on practice in an empirical manner.

There are other forms of theory that seek to explain why something happens. So I want to suggest an addition to Ryle's typology: *knowing why*. The point about this form of knowledge is that it is analytical and framed within the context of systematic academic argument, so that there can be a sociology of adult education and a philosophy of vocational education, and so on, but this is not practical knowledge!

Not every action can be fully explained through articulation: Experts sometimes cannot say precisely how they do something. Ryle makes this point about chess players who cannot always articulate the rules of the game, even when they are playing. They know how to play and they know that certain things cannot be done, but they may not always be able to explain the game. In a recent study about practical knowledge and expertise, Nyiri (1988, pp. 20–21) supports this view (all quotes within this quotation are from Feigenbaum and McCorduck, 1984):

> One becomes an expert not simply by absorbing explicit knowledge of the type found in textbooks, but through experience, that is, through repeated trials, "failing, succeeding, wasting time and effort . . . getting to feel the problem, learning to go by the book and when to break the rules." Human experts thereby gradually absorb "a repertoire of working rules of thumb, or 'heuristics,' that, combined with book

knowledge, make them expert practitioners." This practical, heuristic knowledge, as attempts to simulate it on the machine have shown, is "hardest to get at because experts—or anyone else—rarely have the self-awareness to recognize what it is. So it must be mined out of their heads painstakingly, one jewel at a time."

Ryle may well be correct that some of the original rules are forgotten through constant practice, but Nyiri suggests another element: Through continuous experimentation, new knowledge is gradually absorbed from experience that might never have been articulated. Practical knowledge, then, is hidden in the practitioner, or, as Polyani (1967) suggests, it has become tacit knowledge, that is, knowledge that cannot necessarily be expressed in words. The nature of that knowledge is pragmatic. But because it is known to work, practitioners are loathe to change it. Hence, there appear to be at least two processes of acquiring tacit knowledge: the first is about forgetting and the second is about learning.

Learning Practical Knowledge

We have seen that practical knowledge consists of three elements: knowledge how, knowledge that, and tacit knowledge. Acquisition of the first two occurs through the same processes, and these are not self-evident. Four different processes are discussed here. In addition, there are two processes of acquiring tacit knowledge. Consequently, there are six interrelated processes. They can occur in sequence, although in practice many of them occur simultaneously:

Learning Knowledge How and Knowledge That. This is the type of preparation that occurs in initial professional, or vocational, education. Students attend a training school and are instructed in the knowledge about how to perform in practice. They also learn about what is likely to occur when they perform certain skills, which is knowledge that. This learning may consist of traditional lectures and demonstrations. Knowledge that taught in the classroom should be more specific and relate to actual practice situations. The teaching and learning are often a matter of memorization of material taught and, sometimes, also of the opportunity to practice some of the skills following demonstrations. Ideas such as reflective learning and critical thought are espoused by the teachers, although they may often be rhetoric rather than reality. Indeed, knowledge how and knowledge that are based in practice, and students should be encouraged to test the knowledge before they criticize it! If it works, then it is acceptable; and if it is not practical, then new knowledge and skills have to be created that are more practical. It is in practice that reflective learning should occur, and critical thought should be applied to knowledge why theory. Practical knowledge should be pragmatic, and the opportunity to criticize it should actually occur when it has been tried out in practice.

This characterization has clear implications for teaching, since knowledge how and knowledge that need not be presented within a critical framework. However, it is not knowledge per se that is beyond dispute but rather knowledge that can be tested in practice; its validity lies in its usefulness.

Learning How in Practice. This is the form of knowledge that is gained through doing. It is the type of knowledge that is referred to in the Chinese proverb at the opening of this chapter. Acquisition of this type of knowledge is not necessarily an easy process for a new student, as Mackenzie (1990) showed in her study of how district nursing students (nurses working in the community) learned in their practice setting. Using ethnographical methods, she studied district nursing students undertaking practice and noted that there are three stages in the process. The first she called "fitting in," which is the process of observing how the practice functions and learning from colleagues and senior practitioners—both their strengths and their errors—and then devising strategies that enable them to fit in. The second stage she called "trying and testing out," during which the students moved from dependence on senior practitioners to a level of independence. Finally, the third stage she called "reality of practice," in which the students learn to become practitioners through integration of the practical knowledge learned in the classroom with that learned in practice, where this is possible. Of course, some contradictions are also discovered, and not all of the rules are found to be practicable.

Acquisition of Tacit Knowledge by Forgetting. As Nyiri (1988) pointed out, the independent practitioner begins to forget the original rules. Other writers, such as Ryle (1963) and Benner (1984), make precisely the same point, that with the growth in expertise the original rules tend to play a less conscious part in professional practice. Ryle, for instance, points out that it might be difficult for some expert chess players to articulate the rules of the game, although they would immediately recognize when those rules are being broken. But there is a danger here because this is also the beginning of the process of habitualization, which can also result in bad practice. In this process, however, the theoretical and abstract rules play a less significant part in practice and so they tend to be forgotten. Hence, the knowledge has become internalized, tacit, and difficult for the practitioner to articulate.

Acquisition of Tacit Knowledge by Learning. This is the second element in the process of acquiring tacit knowledge, which starts from two basic assumptions: that practitioners monitor their performances and that they adapt them to different situations. Through this process of conscious action, the actors are learning preconsciously from their practice and skill performance. I discussed preconscious learning in an earlier study (Jarvis, 1987), and it is similar to the process that Marsick and Watkins (1990) call "incidental learning." This process of monitoring and retrospecting on action is totally different from reflective practice, which is discussed in the next subsection. Monitoring and retrospecting on action is a natural process of being consciously aware, even at a very low level of consciousness, of the total situation within which the actions are performed. The results of monitoring and retrospecting on the actions and on any slight adjustments in performance in order to adapt to specific situations are frequently internalized without conscious awareness. Hence, preconscious learning occurs through these processes of thinking about actions, which result in the development of a body of tacit knowledge within practitioners, knowledge that they would find almost impossible to articulate.

Reflective Practice and Knowledge How and Knowledge That. Actors plan, monitor, and retrospect on actions in the normal course of events, but sometimes an action does not produce the expected results; sometimes disjuncture occurs between expectations and achievements. Practitioners cannot always be sure of acting in an almost taken-for-granted manner; they are sometimes confronted with disjuncture and are forced to rethink the whole situation. At this point, practice is the situation in which a reflective learning experience occurs, and if the practitioners reflect on the situation and learn from it, then they add to their body of practical knowledge. Consequently, new skills and new knowledge are being created. This new knowledge might be knowledge how, knowledge that, or a combination of the two. But if the practitioners are too busy, or they reject the opportunity, then nonlearning occurs and their practice will be impoverished because they failed to learn from their experiences.

Knowledge How and Knowledge That and Continuing Learning and Education. Tough (1972) pointed out that many of the self-directed learning projects that he investigated were vocationally oriented. Sargant (1991) discovered the same thing in the United Kingdom, where 9 percent of her sample were individuals studying for vocational qualifications in their leisure time. During this process, practitioners have opportunities to read journals and magazines, there are libraries and learning resource centers available, and there are experts who can be consulted. In addition, there are continuing professional education courses, and these are becoming increasingly available as the growing awareness about human resources development results in more opportunities for additional training. However, the extent to which continuing education, in the more formal sense, relates to the specific learning needs of practice as undertaken by practitioners remains an area in which more research is needed.

Conclusion

Benner (1984), following Dreyfus and Dreyfus (1980), traces five stages in the process from novice to expert: novice, advanced beginner, competent, proficient, and expert. This sequence seems to be a natural progression, but if it were natural and almost inevitable, then every practitioner who stays in practice for a long time would automatically be classified as an expert. However, this is not actually the case, and some people fail to learn from experience. Those long-term practitioners who are not experts may never have achieved that state because they failed to learn from their experiences, and the reasons for nonlearning become increasingly important if human resources are to be developed fully.

But those who are the experts are those who have acquired knowledge how, knowledge that, and tacit knowledge from their practice. It is perhaps even more significant in this age of materialism that only those who are in practice can ever be the experts, for those who leave it cease to be in a position to increase their practical knowledge. Not only is this a lesson for managers, it is also one for teachers! It is only through doing something that a fully developed understanding of it can be acquired, or as Pentti Havukainen (1991, p. 60), a Finnish thinker, wrote, "The best way to understand the tango is to dance it, not analyze it!"

References

Benner, P. *From Novice to Expert: Excellence and Power in Clinical Nursing Practice.* Reading, Mass.: Addison-Wesley, 1984.

Dreyfus, S. E., and Dreyfus, H. *A Five-Stage Model of the Mental Activities Involved in Directed Skill Acquisition.* Berkeley: University of California, 1980.

Feigenbaum, E. A., and McCorduck, P. *The Fifth Generation.* New York: Signet, 1984.

Havukainen, P. "Audio-Education by Bike." *Life and Education in Finland,* 1991, 2, 59–60.

Jarvis, P. *Adult Learning in the Social Context.* London, England: Croom-Helm, 1987.

Jarvis, P. "Practical Knowledge and Theoretical Analyses in Adult and Continuing Education." In M. Friedenthal-Hasse and others (eds.), *Erwachsenenbildung im Kontext* [Adult education in context]. Bad Heilbronn, Germany: Klinkhardt, 1991.

Mackenzie, A. "Learning from Experience in the Community: An Ethnographic Study of District Nurse Students." Unpublished doctoral dissertation, Department of Educational Studies, University of Surrey, England, 1990.

Marsick, V. J., and Watkins, K. E. *Informal and Incidental Learning in the Workplace.* New York: Routledge & Kegan Paul, 1990.

Nyiri, J. C. "Traditional and Practical Knowledge." In J. C. Nyiri and B. Smith (eds.), *Outlines of a Theory of Traditions and Skills.* London, England: Croom-Helm, 1988.

Polyani, M. *The Tacit Dimension.* New York: Routledge & Kegan Paul, 1967.

Ryle, G. *The Concept of Mind.* Harmondsworth, England: Peregrine Books, 1963.

Sargant, N. *Learning and Leisure.* Leicester, England: National Institute of Adult Continuing Education, 1991.

Scheffler, I. *The Conditions of Knowledge.* Chicago: University of Chicago Press, 1965.

Tough, A. *Adults' Learning Projects.* (2nd ed.) Toronto, Ontario, Canada: Ontario Institute for Studies in Education Press, 1979.

PETER JARVIS is professor of continuing education, Department of Educational Studies, University of Surrey, Guildford, Surrey, England.

Examples from various countries and professional fields illustrate societal and organizational influences on professionals' ways of learning that have implications for instruction, program development, and leadership.

Comparative Perspectives on Professionals' Ways of Learning

Alan B. Knox

This chapter reviews international and professional examples that illuminate influences on professionals' ways of learning and provide a comparative perspective to enrich our practice as continuing professional educators. The examples reflect problem-solving strategies (as professionals progress from novice to expert performance) and societal influences (such as organizational dynamics and social change) on learning and performance. Examples from the fields of medicine, teaching, management, and engineering allow comparative analysis across professions.

In our past efforts to strengthen continuing professional education, we focused mainly on learner characteristics (such as abilities, interests, and learning styles). Recently, international perspectives have been especially useful in helping us to understand societal influences on continuing professional education so that we can ask pertinent planning questions in our own national setting. Comparative perspectives across professions in a country help clarify both generic and distinctive features of professional practice. Both learning and occupational performance are influenced by transactions between personal characteristics and situational influences from a dynamic external environment.

The intent of this chapter is to illustrate the types of societal influences on continuing professional education that might be identified by contextual analysis in our own profession and setting. Unfortunately, available examples and research findings are too fragmentary to allow more definitive cross-national and cross-professional conclusions, especially for developing countries.

NEW DIRECTIONS FOR ADULT AND CONTINUING EDUCATION, no. 55, Fall 1992 © Jossey-Bass Publishers

Continuing Education and Professional Expertise

Contextual analysis of societal influences is only one source of insights to strengthen the process and outcomes of continuing professional education by encouraging participation, planning and conducting responsive programs, assessing program impact, and providing strategic leadership. A major objective of continuing education is to enable professionals to progress to higher levels of expertise. This developmental process is affected by self-directed learning activities, along with societal influences. (This interaction of personal and situational influences on enhancement of expertise also applies to practitioners who plan and conduct continuing professional education programs.) Before exploring four categories of societal influences on professional development, I offer the following example of professional development of physicians in technologically advanced countries to illustrate how combinations of education and experience contribute to the development of expertise.

Provocative research findings on medical expertise were reported by a team of scholars from Canada and the Netherlands (Schmidt, Norman, and Boshvizen, 1990). North American studies of expertise indicate similar dynamics in various professional fields (Chi, Glaser, and Farr, 1989). The consensus of these studies is that, at least in technologically advanced countries, progress from novice to expert entails a combination of knowledge and experience relevant to each clinical problem area. Experienced physicians increasingly use indigenous knowledge from experiential learning to create their own cognitive structures (illness scripts) that include scientific generalizations about causes of symptoms but are essentially based on recollections of prototypical and actual patients (and the contexts in which the illnesses occurred). This finding underscores the importance of extensive practical experience as one ingredient in continuing professional education. Under time pressures of actual clinical conditions, experts are able to recall more pertinent knowledge than are novices. As novices become more expert, their clinical reasoning becomes more holistic, and they consider a broader range of situational influences on the problem and its solution, which reflects accumulated indigenous knowledge from experiential learning during clinical practice. This progression is similar to Sternberg's (1988) triarchic theory of intelligence, which is composed of knowledge acquisition, performance, and metacomponents (to plan, monitor, and evaluate problem solving).

In each profession there appear to be field-specific cognitive structures and higher-level concepts (such as illness scripts for physicians) that serve as metacomponents and are used by experts to reflect on combinations of knowledge and experience. These cognitive structures evolve from past professional role performance and constitute the lens through which professionals interpret emerging problems and opportunities.

Political and Economic Trends

Political policies and expectations, along with economic conditions and trends, are especially powerful influences on professional development because they affect priorities and resources for continuing education and the professional field itself. For example, in settings such as developing countries with heavy reliance on government appropriations, a severe economic downturn can sharply reduce continuing education subsidies, support from professionals and their enterprises, and prospects for career advancement.

Similarities and differences regarding continuing engineering education in Japan and the United Kingdom help illuminate societal and organizational influences on professionals' ways of learning. In both countries, comprehensive policies seem desirable to reduce shortages of engineers, including not only policies on continuing education but also policies designed to increase numbers of engineering school graduates, increase attractiveness of incentives, promote technicians, reduce turnover, and reduce recruitment difficulties of enterprises. Compared with the United States, Japan gives more attention to planned change, research and development, and future-oriented training through long-term seniority, job rotation, and group-oriented staff development. By contrast, the United Kingdom emphasizes preparation of individuals for immediate technical problem solving, and promotion to management instead of advancement in technical specialties. In Japan, in contrast with the United Kingdom, there is greater emphasis on personnel development by top management and personnel departments; use of project teams related to research, development, and production; assignment and rotation of engineers to projects to develop abilities; and use of seniority and ability for promotion along specialist career routes comparable in status and salary to managerial progression.

In the United Kingdom, government support consists mainly of encouraging enterprises to increase continuing engineering education, but little or no legislation or direct subsidy. Enterprises have taken the initiative in efforts such as the Professional Industrial and Commercial Updating Program. Economic decline in the United Kingdom stimulated support for continuing engineering education, and demand has increased as reflected in a 1982 regulation requiring individuals to participate in off-site continuing education before taking the final civil engineering professional exam. In most specialties, engineers attend programs with time off and financing from the enterprise. Programs are available from various providers, including associations, enterprises, and higher education institutions. Enterprises are not required to provide continuing education, and some are concerned that engineers who participate in continuing education will be more likely to move to another enterprise.

Staff development in Japan is distinctive in several respects. Japan is one of the seven most industrialized countries in the world and is very competitive technologically. It pioneered W. E. Deming's ideas about use of staff development procedures such as quality circles to achieve quality-improvement goals, long before the United States became interested. At the same time, Japan's Asian cultural values include group solidarity versus the individualism of the West, lifetime employment practices in large enterprises (which account for about 25 percent of the work force), and advancement and pay based mainly on seniority (which shifts the emphasis of staff development from individual advancement to long-term enterprise productivity and reduces staff resistance to technology for fear of displacement). Small- and medium-size enterprises without the capability for extensive internal staff development use government-sponsored adult vocational education institutes and sometimes the staff development programs of larger enterprises (similar to staff development provided by the large U.S. accounting firms for members of smaller firms). However, social and economic changes have resulted in recent gradual changes in the employment system to emphasize merit for promotion, in contrast to traditional reliance on seniority. Extensive and varied staff development has evolved that reflects the Japanese cultural context, including emphasis on teamwork, job rotation, cross-training, career paths, and, in general, long-term productivity and the competitive position of enterprises.

Government influence is especially evident in an example from Ireland, in which the Health Education Bureau of the national government established a high priority for in-service education of secondary school teachers by influencing policy and plans and providing full funding. The program reflects collaboration between the bureau and local schools, and, in addition to bureau priorities, program policies were responsive to increasing public concern about health and feedback from earlier program participants. Staffing decisions were influenced by bureau financial arrangements, but also by local schools and by evidence of outcomes. Participation by teachers (as students in the program) was influenced by anticipated benefits, collaboration with the schools, and some evidence of actual outcomes (Knox, in press).

In Greece, in-service education of elementary and secondary school teachers reflects fragmented and limited provision of adult education generally, political and economic turmoil, and classical versus vocational emphasis on preparatory education. Recent efforts to implement proposals to reform in-service education for teachers by establishing quasi-independent regional teacher centers—publicly financed but with shared governance among representatives of teachers' unions, schools, and universities (Knox, in press)—were delayed by economic and political problems. Earlier programs sponsored by the government were held in few locations (which discouraged participation) and had centralized priorities (which emphasized transmission of classical knowledge).

In some African countries, such as Ghana and Nigeria, in which primary and secondary education is mainly a national or provincial government responsibility, efforts to increase access to preparatory education by young people are restricted by limited support for in-service education of too few and underqualified teachers (Knox, in press). The minimal support of in-service educational opportunities for individual teachers reflects limited resources, too many young students, too few qualified teachers, barriers to in-service education in rural areas, government priorities, and decisions that favor numbers reached more than program impact.

In Sweden, recent exploration of policy alternatives regarding occupational adult education considered various combinations of public-sector and enterprise contributions. A promising alternative is the concept of a learning enterprise in which comprehensive policies of government, enterprises, and educational institutions give attention to economic development and job design, as well as to collaboration, educational leave, and time for studies as an inherent part of a job. This concept of workplaces as both productive and learning enterprises fits well with Swedish adult education policy, which promotes an educative society (Abrahamsson, 1990; Abrahamsson, Hultinger, and Svenningsson, 1990).

New Knowledge and Technology

The second category of societal influence on professional learning is professionals' perceptions of the base and rate of change in new knowledge and technology. Especially in technologically advanced countries, this influence is typically thought of as obsolescence (due to social change, research, innovation, and changes in organizational arrangements and relations with clients), with technology transfer and updates as the appropriate continuing education response (Cervero, 1988; Willis, Dubin, and Associates, 1990). By contrast, attention to appropriate technology and indigenous knowledge in some developing countries and professional specialties in the West reflect an appreciation of value judgments regarding local benefits and life-styles, with continuing education designed to help professionals improve their service through access to knowledge resource systems, instead of dissemination of new knowledge and technology as the goal.

Technology transfer can entail organizational as well as personal change, as illustrated by the computerization of paper mills in the United States (Zuboff, 1988). Prior to computerization, traditional paper mill managers and operators functioned in an action-centered oral culture, in which staff members thought in a present-tense flow of action with little time devoted to deliberate reflection. Crucial knowledge was indigenous, arose from accumulated experience, was transmitted through an oral culture, and was difficult to codify. Much of staff development was coaching and on-the-job training. Compared with implicit authority of managers and tacit knowledge of operators before computerization, afterward there was more abstract and reflective reasoning based on symbolic mastery and explicitly constructed meanings. Computerization brought many changes, including increased pace of change, fewer staff members, decline in social exchange, disruption of role identity, and a shift from individual to team cooperation and problem solving based on public data. Computerization also made the organization more transparent, increased the intellectual content of work, reduced former distinctions between manager and operator roles, and modified managers' ways of learning and performing.

Prior to computerization, transcendent enterprise values and specialized education gave managers authority, and the resultant private knowledge gave managers power and control, which helped maintain distance from operators. Computerization increased and changed interaction between managers and operators by challenging managerial authority, status differentials, and unilateral surveillance. The most dramatic shift related to successful computerization was that managers moved from directing performance to directing learning. In this instance, the introduction of new technology triggered more reflection by managers and other staff members on decision making, values, and organizational relations.

Work Settings

The third category of influence on professional learning is the organizational setting in which practice occurs. Increasingly in technologically advanced countries, professionals work in large collective or hierarchical organizations with selection criteria, performance standards, career paths, and interpersonal tensions. This setting contrasts with the settings of many professionals in developing countries whose work relationships are akin to extended families. However, because of the sparcity of analyses of the effects of work setting on professional learning in developing countries, this section focuses on Western examples (Knox, in press). In the United States, practice standards and quality improvement are major organizational influences on professional learning in the health professions. A central organizational issue pertains to the influences of staff roles related to individual advancement and organizational productivity on in-service education.

For professionals in a hierarchical setting, their ways of learning are affected by their interactions with other organization members in staff development, whether for teachers in schools, nurses in hospitals, engineers in factories, or supervisors in enterprises (Cervero, 1988; Houle, 1980). Staff development conducted by administrators for school teachers occurs in many countries, but in the United States local school boards and administrators are a distinctive source of influence in the name of accountability for program quality (Knox, in press).

Comprehension of the purposes of staff development (including career-long formal and informal learning activities) can help teachers and administrators who plan in-service activities to differentiate among the needs of teachers at different career stages. Some beginning teachers have been characterized as anticipatory in approach, with energy and interest in innovation. Consequently, the large majority of passive participants in required in-service sessions are composed of accomplished master teachers, who continue to progress on their own, and of others who can be characterized as adequate followers, dependent on context and the expectations of others. Another stage consists of reticent teachers, which includes withdrawn and sometimes obstructionist teachers who often expend more energy on resisting change than on improving their performance, along with teachers preparing for retirement. Effective staff development activities sometimes manage to move teachers who are withdrawn and passive regarding in-service activities into a career renewal stage. The norms and culture of a school system influence the vitality of staff development, as reflected in the contrasting influence on teacher motivation to participate in staff development activities in a school where peers are enthusiastic about innovation and growth versus a school where peers resist change.

A major criterion for success of teacher development is impact on student achievement, but it has been difficult to evaluate this influence because in-service activity is but one of many influences on achievement. As a result, attention is given to intermediary characteristics of teaching and learning that staff development could enhance and that are likely to increase achievement. Examples include teacher sense of efficacy, high but realistic expectations for student performance, a supportive classroom climate for learning, waiting after asking student questions, and especially high student time spent on learning tasks.

A long-standing but recently refined form of staff development associated with improved teacher performance is clinical supervision, in which supervisor and teacher discuss a class session to be observed by the supervisor, who notes teacher and student behavior, which they discuss later and, on the basis of the teacher's performance, plan future instructional activities. This association between performance, feedback, and improvement has also been demonstrated in relation to microteaching. The benefits of clinical supervision depend on a satisfactory working relationship between supervisor and teacher because, in many instances, teachers perceive postobservation conferences as unproductive and supervisors as artificial and threatening. By contrast, successful conferences encourage teachers to engage in productive innovation and goal setting. Peer coaching is a similar procedure in which experienced teachers observe each other's classrooms and then discuss their observations with varying degrees of feedback. Evaluation demonstrates that coaching results in improved teaching and student performance (Joyce and Showers, 1988; Joyce, Bennett, and Rolhelser-Bennett, 1990; Schein, 1978).

Enterprise staff development is distinctively positioned to emphasize application because of concern for individual staff development and enterprise productivity. One approach that emphasizes application is action learning (Marsick, 1987; Marsick and Watkins, 1990; Pedler, 1983). Action learning projects are mainly planned and implemented by one or a small group of staff members, and the goals are improved performance at individual, group, organizational, or occupational levels. By focusing on a desirable improvement related to enterprise functioning, the staff member engages in an action learning project that involves other staff members who have a stake in the improvement, and as a result learning and action become complementary parts of the process. Over the years, similar concepts and procedures have been termed action research, organization development, action science, and participatory research. All share basic concepts such as active participation by learners, including diagnosis of current performance and content; attention to desirability of goals; planning and evaluation of learning activities and impact on organization; explicit attention to application; and seminar sessions to help action learners reflect on the process (Argyris, Putnam, and Smith, 1985).

Action learning for managers with international responsibilities provides an excellent example of a staff development approach initiated in the United Kingdom and adapted for use in Sweden and the United States. Managers engage in action learning to refine their personal models of leadership through combinations of actual projects, seminar participation, personal reflection, and exchange of perspectives with peers and experts. The goal is to help managers become holistic, strategic thinkers who use solid judgment in detecting problems and implementing solutions as well as in decision making in self-renewing learning enterprises in which staff members assume mutual responsibility for creation and achievement of goals. The action learning process has evolved differently in the United Kingdom, United States, Sweden, and Japan to reflect each societal context and has been especially valuable in helping managers with internal responsibilities to appreciate cross-national differences in the influence of organizational and national culture and values on work and education (Marsick and Cederholm, 1988; Marsick and Watkins, 1990; Revans, 1971).

Some staff development activities in various countries focus on cross-cultural understandings, which have become especially important to the increasing number of staff members in enterprises with international dealings, and even in domestic enterprises in which managers deal with contrasting subcultures in the work force. Studies of international differences in organizational values and behavior have implications for both management and training (Adler, 1991; Bellah and Associates, 1985). American cultural orientations have been characterized as individualistic, private, and action-oriented in the present or near future, in contrast with other cultural orientations characterized by greater value on group, public, and past activities. Cross-cultural differences also are apparent in regard to status differentials and avoidance of uncertainty. Staff development activities have been increasingly provided to help staff members understand and deal effectively with cultural value differences, both internationally and for domestic subcultures.

Hofstede's (1980) extensive cross-national study of work-related values identified cultural differences with major implications for continuing education of managers. Cross-national differences (regarding such cultural characteristics as individualism, avoidance of uncertainty, and power differentials) affected management development activities in the context of enterprise and national subcultures. Especially in enterprises with international connections, effective managers sought to understand local contingencies as they promoted organizational development to achieve teamwork and shared visions. Hofstede concluded that organizational development efforts to stimulate interpersonal openness and feedback, which were effective in the United States but were somewhat less effective in the United Kingdom, tended to be dependent on authority in France, to be considered distractions from task achievement in Germany, to be subversive in Latin America, and to risk embarrassment in Japan. These findings underscore the importance of contingency leadership based on understanding of cultural values as an important feature of the continuing education of managers who interact with people from various subcultures in the United States as well as in other countries. The increasing prominence of the European Economic Community in 1992, the emergence of other common market arrangements elsewhere, and the increased extent of multinational enterprises underscore the growing importance of understanding cross-national aspects of professionals' ways of learning.

Opportunity System

The fourth category of influences is professionals' opportunity systems. These influences occur as learners deal with life space demands and constraints as they select and sequence learning activities from multiple providers of continuing education. A professional's opportunity system reflects characteristics such as learning ability, educational level, occupational values, status, subculture, affluence, sense of proficiency, learning style, access to colleagues and resources, and incentives and benefits of professional development. Demands and constraints associated with work, family, and community affect continuing education goals and the methods that professionals select. Consider contrasting examples of an isolated rural professional in solo practice, where participation entails high costs associated with being away from work and family, and a similar professional in an urban group practice, where participation can be integrated with peer interaction (Fox, Maxmanian, and Putnam, 1989; Knox, 1990).

In technologically advanced countries, multiple continuing education providers enable professionals to select learning activities that fit their needs, circumstances, and preferred learning styles. Professionals from developing countries have attended programs transplanted from other countries where advances occur more rapidly, which can disconnect them from local realities.

The availability of multiple providers also leads to program accreditation in the interest of quality and responsiveness, and collaboration in the interest of complementarity among providers. An example of complementarity among providers is program cosponsorship by a university teaching hospital where professors of medicine are willing to conduct programs in cosponsoring community hospitals for the convenience of local physicians, who (if the program is beneficial) may refer their patients in need of specialized care to the teaching hospital, on which the professors' research and teaching depend (Knox, 1982).

Professional characteristics and multiple educational resources can encourage self-directedness, in which professionals develop personalized professional development strategies composed of sequences of educational activities from various sources (Means, 1984). A professional's active search for meaning through a sequence of learning activities entails selection from available learning activities, such as reading, professional meetings, continuing education courses and workshops, and especially workplace learning (Candy, 1991; Hiemstra and Sisco, 1990; Merriam and Caffarella, 1991; Owen, Allery, Harding, and Hayes, 1989; Knox, 1985, 1990; Schein, 1978; Smith and Associates, 1990).

Implications for Practice

A cross-national and cross-professional comparative perspective can enable planners to recognize important societal and organizational influences in their own context. The following are illustrative implications based on the four categories of influence reviewed in this chapter: (1) Recognition of political and economic trends emphasizes the importance of leadership to involve a broad range of stakeholders in strategic planning to strengthen program development and administration. Attention to societal influences should help ensure multiple sources of financial support. (2) Attention to emerging knowledge and technology related to a professional field can be used to strengthen instruction and encourage participation in educational programs that explore indigenous knowledge and appropriate technology as well as update new developments. (3) Analysis of work settings as learning enterprises can be used to guide program development that is responsive to both individual career advancement and organizational productivity. (4) Appreciation of the relative abundance of opportunity systems can contribute to program coordination that considers multiple providers and encourages active learning in activities that are responsive to local circumstances such as competing expectations and access to resources as well as preferred learning style.

References

Abrahamsson, K. *Learning Rights for the Next Century: Improving Learning Options by a New Deal Between the Public and Private Interests in Adult Learning.* Stockholm, Sweden: Division of Adult Education, Swedish National Board of Education, 1990.

Abrahamsson, K., Hultinger, E., and Svenningsson, L. *Expanding Learning Enterprises in Sweden.* Stockholm, Sweden: Swedish National Board of Education, 1990.

Adler, N. J. *International Dimensions of Organizational Behavior.* (2nd ed.) Belmont, Calif.: Wadsworth, 1991.

Argyris, C., Putnam, R., and Smith, D. M. *Action Science: Concepts, Methods, and Skills for Research and Intervention.* San Francisco: Jossey-Bass, 1985.

Bellah, R. N., and Associates. *Habits of the Heart.* New York: HarperCollins, 1985.

Candy, P. C. *Self-Direction for Lifelong Learning: A Comprehensive Guide to Theory and Practice.* San Francisco: Jossey-Bass, 1991.

Cervero, R. M. *Effective Continuing Education for Professionals.* San Francisco: Jossey-Bass, 1988.

Chi, M.T.H., Glaser, R., and Farr, M. J. *The Nature of Expertise.* Hillsdale, N.J.: Erlbaum, 1989.

Fox, R. D., Mazmanian, P. E., and Putnam, R. W. (eds.). *Changing and Learning in the Lives of Physicians.* New York: Praeger, 1989.

Hiemstra, R., and Sisco, B. *Individualizing Instruction: Making Learning Personal, Empowering, and Successful.* San Francisco: Jossey-Bass, 1990.

Hofstede, G. *Culture's Consequences: International Differences in Work-Related Values.* Newbury Park, Calif.: Sage, 1980.

Houle, C. O. *Continuing Learning in the Professions.* San Francisco: Jossey-Bass, 1980.

Joyce, B., Bennett, B., and Rolhelser-Bennett, C. "The Self-Educating Teacher: Empowering Teachers Through Research." In B. Joyce (ed.), *The 1990 ASCD Yearbook: Changing School Culture Through Staff Development.* Alexandria, Va.: Association for Supervision and Curriculum Development, 1990.

Joyce, B., and Showers, B. *Student Achievement Through Staff Development.* White Plains, N.Y.: Longman, 1988.

Knox, A. B. "Organizational Dynamics in University Continuing Professional Education." *Adult Education,* 1982, 32 (3), 117–129.

Knox, A. B. "Adult Learning and Proficiency." In D. Kleiber and M. Maehr (eds.), *Motivation in Adulthood.* Advances in Motivation and Achievement, vol. 4. Greenwood, Conn.: JAI Press, 1985.

Knox, A. B. "Influences on Continuing Education Participation." *Journal of Continuing Education in the Health Professions,* 1990, *10* (3), 261–274.

Knox, A. B. *Strengthening Continuing Education: A World Perspective on Synergistic Leadership.* San Francisco: Jossey-Bass, in press.

Marsick, V. J. (ed.). *Learning in the Workplace.* London, England: Croom-Helm, 1987.

Marsick, V. J., and Cederholm, L. "Developing Leadership in International Managers—An Urgent Challenge!" *Columbia Journal of World Business,* 1988, *23* (4), 3–11.

Marsick, V. J., and Watkins, K. E. *Informal and Incidental Learning in the Workplace.* New York: Routledge & Kegan Paul, 1990.

Means, R. P. "How Family Physicians Use Information Sources: Implications for New Approaches." In J. S. Green, S. J. Grosswald, E. Suter, and D. B. Walthall III (eds.), *Continuing Education for the Health Professions: Developing, Managing, and Evaluating Programs for Maximum Impact on Patient Care.* San Francisco: Jossey-Bass, 1984.

Merriam, S. B., and Caffarella, R. S. *Learning in Adulthood: A Comprehensive Guide.* San Francisco: Jossey-Bass, 1991.

Owen, P. A., Allery, L. A., Harding, K. G., and Hayes, T. M. "General Practitioners' Continuing Medical Education Within and Outside Their Practice." *British Medical Journal,* 1989, *299,* 238–240.

Pedler, M. (ed.). *Action Learning in Practice.* Aldershot, Hants, England: Gower, 1983.

Revans, R. W. *Developing Effective Managers: A New Approach to Business Education.* New York: Praeger, 1971.

Schein, E. H. *Career Dynamics: Managing Individual and Organizational Needs.* Reading, Mass.: Addison-Wesley, 1978.

Schmidt, H. G., Norman, G. R., and Boshvizen, H.P.A. "A Cognitive Perspective on Medical Expertise: Theory and Implications." *Academic Medicine,* 1990, *65* (10), 611–621.

Smith, R. M., and Associates. *Learning to Learn Across the Life Span.* San Francisco: Jossey-Bass, 1990.

Sternberg, R. J. *The Triarchic Mind: A New Theory of Human Intelligence.* New York: Viking Penguin, 1988.

Willis, S. L., and Dubin, S. S., and Associates. *Maintaining Professional Competence: Approaches to Career Enhancement, Vitality, and Success Throughout a Work Life.* San Francisco: Jossey-Bass, 1990.

Zuboff, S. *In the Age of the Smart Machine.* New York: Basic Books, 1988.

ALAN B. KNOX *is professor of continuing education, University of Wisconsin, Madison.*

Given the growing discrepancy between emerging paradigms about professional learning and actual practice, what can practitioners do about it?

Putting Theory to Practice and Practice to Theory

H. K. Morris Baskett, Victoria J. Marsick, Ronald M. Cervero

We begin this chapter by identifying some of the polar perspectives presented in this volume. We then look at a number of directions that continuing professional educators might take to resolve these tensions. We conclude by examining some of the forces that make it difficult for those involved in the professional education system to adopt the needed strategies and approaches.

Polar Issues in Professional Learning and Change

As we look back on the content of this book, it is apparent that the contributors are struggling with a number of issues. We see these as polarities or tensions that we are experiencing generally in the field of professional learning and continuing professional education (CPE). These polar issues include the following:

Individual Versus Collective. To what degree do professionals work and learn in isolation? To what degree do they learn with and through colleagues and clients as they make sense of their practice?

Rational Versus Intuitive. To what extent do professionals learn through clearly reasoned, explicitly stated thinking? To what degree is learning influenced by the intuitive leaps and implicit understandings that are not always amenable to rational analysis?

Cognitive Versus Emotional. When and how do emotions shape learning that has heretofore been considered primarily cognitive?

Routine Versus Nonroutine. To what extent can learning dilemmas be mapped out, predicted, expected, and hence taught by examining the

New Directions for Adult and Continuing Education, no. 55, Fall 1992 © Jossey-Bass Publishers

known repertoire of professional experience? To what extent are a large percentage of the situations faced nonroutine and hence unsolvable through codified expert knowledge?

Formal Versus Informal. To what extent does structured, designed, accredited planned education contribute to professionals' ways of knowing? To what extent does learning from experience contribute?

Constructed Versus Scientific Knowledge. Is professional knowledge gained through the discovery of inviolable principles and rules, which are then formally codified and applied? Is professional knowledge socially and culturally constructed and context specific?

In practice, these are not opposite perspectives; rather, they overlap and interact. More often than not, writers in CPE unquestioningly assume models of professional learning that tend to be closer to one side of these constructs than the other. Rarely are these issues contrasted in the literature so that the reader can understand the underlying suppositions of a particular model.

Heeding the Lessons: Options for Continuing Professional Educators

Revisions in our understanding of how professionals learn may require subsequent adjustments in how we facilitate that learning. It would be misleading to indulge in prescriptive hyperbole; we do not have, nor will we probably ever have, simple formulas that clearly tell continuing professional educators how they must now function. We do, however, have general suggestions arising from the work contained in this volume, from other literature, and from experience. And these ideas can help those involved in the education of professionals to choose the best paths in developing professionals who are able to make wise and effective decisions. Some of these suggestions directly derive from the tensions outlined above. Others derive from what is not said but is implicit in many of the observations in this book.

Mind Our Business. The first suggestion is not new but bears repeating: Be clear about the nature of our business. We are in the learning business, not the education business. If we see ourselves as being in the education business, we may have predetermined our responses because education, including adult education, has developed a limited repertoire of technologies and approaches with which to respond to any situation, somewhat analogous to the phrase "Give a boy a hammer, and everything becomes a nail!"

By keeping in mind that we are in the learning business, we can pay attention to how professionals actually learn—the focus of this book— and how we might help to improve these learning processes. We may then choose from a wider range of potential responses such as promoting

coaching and mentoring, influencing how preprofessional training occurs, assisting in the restructuring of how professionals interact with
society and clients, and helping to make the procedures of mandatory
continuing education more effective.

These responses frame a particular conceptualization of what continuing professional educators do. It is not sufficient to be a technician, a
kind of unthinking purveyor of the program planning cycle. Abilities to
help bring about social change and personal transformation are also
required. Professionals need help in working through what are often
immense and all-encompassing changes. Louise, a lawyer discussed by
Loughlin and Mott (Chapter Eight), decided that the underlying assumptions of the laws designed to protect battered women were part of the
problem. This led her to enter politics, because that is where she could be
most effective in making significant changes. This decision involved
more than simply learning about a new technology or technique; it
involved her total person in redefining what the issue was, how it could
be tackled, and how it affected her own values and authenticity.

Continuing professional educators must assist professionals as they
ask themselves about their own authenticity and commitment. Just as we
in CPE need to remind ourselves of what business we are in, our clients,
the professionals, also need help in minding their business. Being a professional means much more than simply providing a service to a client. A
professional must ask if there are alternate ways of solving an issue or
problem; in essence, a professional is, ideally, a good critical thinker.

**Work Toward a More Holistic Approach to Improving Professional
Learning.** Several of the chapters in this volume either directly or indirectly view professional learning as involving all aspects of human existence. It is clearly fallacious to assume that professional learning occurs
in isolation. Colleagues, clients, family and friends, as well as many
others influence the way in which professionals learn and change, as
Parochka and Fox (1989) reported in their study of physicians. Paul and
Osborne (1989) found sixty-six episodes of change that were ascribed to
relationships with other physicians.

The women about which Loughlin and Mott write learned much by
interacting with one another, and by connecting the themes in their lives
with social forces—based on race, gender, and class—that constrain as
well as trigger learning. One set of themes raised by their discussion is
how technical, instrumental knowledge, embodied in rational systems of
thought, can be blended with intuitive knowing, which may emerge from
holistic systems of thinking or being. CPE focuses primarily on the
cognitive dimensions of learning to the exclusion of affective concerns.
Yet, these latter play a strong role in professional service and in the way
in which many professionals learn. Boreham (Chapter Seven), too, calls
our attention to the role of the nonrational in professional learning and

practice in his discussion of implicit knowledge in medicine. Gender concerns are often linked with this discussion, as is a questioning of the positivist paradigm of scientific research. Many of the studies discussed at the Professionals' Ways of Knowing conference in Montreal, for example, were based on in-depth qualitative analyses of contextual factors in relation to professional learning. Storytelling emerged as an important tool both for knowing and for passing on the lessons of the culture to new professionals.

One of the key implications of this work is the need for new models that take into account transformative learning, learning through relationships, intuitive knowing, the affective dimension of learning, and situational variables. For continuing professional educators, this can mean intervening to redesign physical space so that interaction and learning occur more naturally among professionals; encouraging organizations in which professionals work to maximize the learning opportunities available in various meetings; legitimizing self-help, peer support, and counseling for professionals as an aid to transformative learning; and helping to leverage the learning potential of peer and performance reviews.

Build Better Preprofessional Programs. Much of the criticism about professional education addresses the inadequacy of the early training of professionals. Farquharson (1983) has advocated training preprofessionals in a variety of self-directed learning skills. McMaster University, in Hamilton, Ontario, Canada, has developed a much-studied self-directed program for medical students that builds skills in learning self-sufficiency. Others have advocated removing professional schools from university settings, where the emphasis is on conceptual knowledge, to training institutes, where the emphasis is on practical knowledge.

It may seem a daunting task to those involved in preprofessional education to restructure basic professional degree training. Nonetheless, educators of professionals can make an impact through the use of conferences, professional journals, and action groups to help stimulate the examination of present preprofessional educational systems and the consideration of other possibilities. It is important, too, to sensitize decision makers to alternative ways of learning and understanding, and to incorporate these alternatives into the educational process. Benner (1984) in nursing and Grimmett and MacKinnon (1992) in teaching explore ways in which "working knowledge" can be incorporated into professional preparation.

Move to Where the Learning Occurs, Create Systems for Just-in-Time Learning. As many of the studies described in this book attest, a very large portion of professional learning occurs during practice of one's profession. It seems reasonable, therefore, to suggest that learning facilitators situate themselves at those action points. This does not mean that every professional needs a shadow educator; rather, it means that continuing professional educators need to strategize to maximize the learning potential of the situation. Often, this approach involves equipping those who interact with professionals—other professionals, supervisors, and managers—with the tools needed to understand the learning act and to assist each other in learning from experience as well as learning how to learn from experience.

It is not always possible to have all knowledge about all things available when a professional needs it. Even if this was possible, professionals need to reflect on the consequences of the information that they receive, and they are not always able to digest just-in-time professional information. Consequently, they need to develop their search, retrieval, problem-solving, and reflection skills.

Nonetheless, the availability of the right resources at the right time is a valuable aspect of effective professional learning and decision making. Jennett and Pearson (Chapter Three) describe how a number of telephone and computer-accessed information systems, based on physicians' real-time problems, can help in the effective treatment of patients by medical practitioners in outlying areas. The design and testing of such systems is a central challenge for educators of professionals.

Legitimize and Pay Greater Attention to Practical Knowledge. Over the past century, universities have supplanted places of practice such as agencies, law offices, and hospitals as the generators and repositories of professional knowledge (Resnik, 1987; Clifford and Guthrie, 1988). In the process, practical, or "craft," knowledge developed from experience has been replaced by abstract, academic, and codified knowledge. Practical knowledge, in effect, has become delegitimized.

Cervero (1992) has argued for a "reclaiming" of practical knowledge as a legitimate and worthwhile part of professional knowing. In this volume, Jarvis (Chapter Nine) points to the importance of practical knowledge and suggests that it involves several levels of complexity: knowledge how, knowledge that, and tacit knowledge that is buried in expert practice.

In order to help reclaim craft knowledge, Cervero (1992) suggests that continuing educators must first help professionals to realize the nature, extent, and importance of the practical knowledge that they possess and then assist them in making this knowledge explicit. This task is as important as the task of helping them to develop and learn new knowledge.

A cautionary note is in order, however. In making this knowledge explicit, we must recognize that professionals are reporting social constructions of reality, and that their experiences are subject to the limits of what can be expressed in language. Hunt (1987) suggests that professionals hold their theories of practice up for public and collegial scrutiny and be ready to revise these practice theories in the light of alternate perspectives and new data.

In addition to helping professionals articulate and legitimize their repertoires of practical knowledge, continuing professional educators should help professionals understand the processes by which they use practical knowledge in their practice contexts. This calls for a departure from the prevailing assumptions imbedded in CPE practice, that is, what the learner does is more important than what the instructor does. As observed in Chapter One here, learning is internal to the learner. CPE practitioners need to enable professionals to observe, engage in, and discover their own kinds of thinking in action. As Brown, Collins, and Duguid (1989) and Collins, Brown, and Newman (1989) point out, this assistance will permit them to see if this kind of knowing fits with their abstract knowledge and how they make use of a variety of resources in their social and physical environment.

Cervero (1992) proposes a typology, based on work by Collins, Brown, and Newman (1989), by which professionals can be helped to gain practical knowledge. Farmer, Buckmaster, and LeGrand (Chapter Four) suggest a similar typology. In order to help practitioners develop their craft knowledge in areas in which they are unfamiliar, observation and guided and supported practice are recommended. Modeling, coaching (Schön, 1987; Yakowicz, 1987), and scaffolding are effective interventions to achieve this end. As Farmer, Buckmaster, and LeGrand detail in terms of cognitive apprenticeship, scaffolding is particularly useful with ill-defined, risky, and complex problems.

To help professionals gain conscious access to, and control of, their own knowledge and reasoning processes as well as those of experts, articulation and reflection are recommended. Journal writing, conversations with experts (McAlpine, Frew, and Lucas, 1991), and reflective problem solving with more experienced practitioners are very good ways of accessing these imbedded knowledge processes.

To encourage learner autonomy in defining and formulating problems to be solved, exploration is suggested, whereby the practitioner practices on her or his own but has expert backup. Farmer, Buckmaster, and LeGrand's description of how pharmacists are introduced to new techniques is a concrete example of how exploration might work in practice.

We are not suggesting that practical knowledge is all that is needed for effective professional practice, and that abstract, codified, and declarative knowing has no contribution to make. As both Abbott (1988) and Hunt (1987) remind us, the two are really complementary. Underlying regularities that seem nonsensical within practical knowledge can be revealed through systematic study and the use of codified knowledge and principles. Moreover, exclusive focus on practical knowledge and reasoning simply because it is used in daily practice can lead to the mistaken belief that the way things are is the way that they ought to be. The challenge to professionals, and to those who assist them in maintaining and improving their competence, is to integrate abstract and practical knowledge and reasoning in such a way that it leads to wiser professional actions.

Address Contextual Influences on Professional Learning. Professionals are characterized in much of the literature as having relatively high levels of autonomy; there is an expectation that they will make judgments independently, after a careful consideration of the facts of the situation. CPE models have been based on the assumption that professionals prefer to learn as they were trained: individually, or in groups, but without emphasizing the connection that individuals have with one another in their real work contexts. Efforts to help professionals learn on their own support the inference that they prefer individualized learning modes, as we see in the work by Klevans, Smutz, Shuman, and Bershad (Chapter Two) and in many of the modes available to medically based learners described by Jennett and Pearson (Chapter Three).

However, as Nowlen (1988) points out, professional services are also carried out in conjunction with many other providers within settings that reflect many diverse cultures: those of the providers, the clients, and the organizations and communities through which service is enacted. Professional decisions and learning are carried out within specific contexts and will vary from context to context. And yet, the milieu of CPE, the cultures of the service systems within which professionals work, and many of the national cultures that have spawned professional knowledge do not always support this kind of contextual knowing and learning.

Knox (Chapter Ten) speaks to the many social, political, organizational, and economic factors that impact on the way in which CPE is delivered. As he points out, many of his examples come from Western countries—cultures that Hofstede's (1980) research on cultural values suggests are more likely to be individualistic. The examples in which there is concern for the community come from Scandinavia, which Hofstede found to be more collectively conscious.

Research into how professionals learn in non-Western cultures should help us to understand through contrast the dynamics of professional knowing. For Western countries, this understanding is especially critical because not only are the population mixes becoming more culturally and ethnically diverse, but the composition of the professions is similarly becoming more diverse. On the other hand, professional training and knowledge frequently emanate from Western knowledge bases that have been shared across national boundaries with urban, educated elites who speak Western languages, work in multi- or cross-national contexts, and may be culturally attuned to Euro-American perspectives.

The women's literature also raises many questions about learning from and through others. Lovin's (Chapter Six) work on paraprofessionals speaks to the value of relationships for learning, but she also describes the way in which the environment and the nature of the work itself supports or inhibits learning. Ellerington, Marsick, and Dechant's (Chapter Five) story of Imperial Oil addresses both the individualized learning needs of people working on their own and a collective, networked learning process within an organization. Questions can be raised about the autonomy of the learners in the story, and the role of the organization in influencing the directions of their learning. However, the Imperial Oil story shows that environments can be created that foster continuous learning at many levels.

Factors That Make Change Difficult

We have made the case that those of us who are in the business of educating professionals should reexamine the business we are in. However, as we all know, this is more easily said than done. A number of forces work against changing our practices, and these need to be identified and integrated into our strategies to bring about change.

Lack of Knowledge. Many educators of professionals do not know that new understandings are emerging that are drastically revising our outlook and practice possibilities; consequently, they cannot change their practices. Professional school educators' energies are usually directed toward developing expertise in their particular subject matter, whether litigation law or counseling theory. This in itself is a full-time job. Little time or energy is left to study how one develops professionals who understand the learning process. Similarly, those involved in CPE and the facilitation of professional competence are under pressure to meet program and budget targets and lack time and energy to focus on recent research and its implications for their practices.

Lack of Practice-Related Knowledge. Continuing professional educators feel bombarded by the rash of new studies and concepts now being published, and although they work hard to remain current in their fields, they often lose interest in trying to make practice sense out of these disparate and sometimes contradictory studies. This is especially true because much of the literature that they read is in the form of narrow reports of research or debates among academics. Analysis and distillation of research about a particular problem take years, and getting a practical book published and in the hands of practitioners takes even longer.

Greater efforts are needed to ensure that practitioners and researchers work together to produce research that meets the needs of practitioners and the field. Action research, participatory and collaborative research, and mutual inquiry approaches are designs that hold promise to meet these needs.

Organizational and Institutional Forces. People responsible for the continuing development and competence of professionals usually work within organizations—professional associations, corporations, colleges and universities, and governments. As Schön (1983) and Calderhead (1988) have pointed out, these organizations typically assume that professional knowledge can be taught context-free as universal or standardized principles. This simple assumption means that a certain implicit theory of knowledge, or epistemology, dominates many institutions and their practices. For example, most professional schools believe that a basic grounding in science and the arts is necessary, because the general concepts and principles can be built on and imported into professional schools and subsequently into professional practices. The apprenticeship approach in professional development has until very recently been undervalued, and university knowledge has been prized as the only valid way of understanding.

Professional and educational organizations have a stake in the present approaches to education. Over a period of time, huge investments of time, energy, and commitment to certain methodologies and technologies, including distance education, electronic classrooms, and instructional technology, have served to entrench these approaches. In effect, this powerful and growing system of preparatory education and CPE has taken on a life of its own, almost separate from the issues of professional learning and change. Complete departments in industry, government, and academia are given over to professional education. The norms and demands of these organizations influence the educational approaches of professional educators and trainers. Balanced budgets, increased volume of output, and faster results have tended to replace competence and effective learning as goals. In relentlessly working to improve the present technologies and approaches, we have not often paused to ask if they are now taking us where we need to go. Given the difficulty in clearly measuring the effects of professional education and training, we are at times in danger of substituting efficiency and productivity for efficacy.

The present system of education for professionals involves more than training and educational groups. It involves public policymakers, individual professionals, education providers and consultants, and professional associations as well. This system has become so integrated and symbiotic, with many cross-linked associations and internal rewards, that it is able to sustain itself, almost without due regard to whether the ultimate client—the patient, client, or customer—is benefiting.

References

Abbott, A. *The System of Professions.* Chicago: University of Chicago Press, 1988.

Benner, P. *From Novice to Expert: Excellence and Power in Clinical Nursing Practice.* Reading, Mass.: Addison-Wesley, 1984.

Brown, J. S., Collins, A., and Duguid, P. "Situated Cognition and the Culture of Learning." *Educational Researcher,* 1989, *18,* 32–42.

Calderhead, J. (ed.). *Teachers' Professional Learning.* London, England: Falmer Press, 1988.

Cervero, R. M. "Professional Practice, Learning, and Continuing Education: An Integrated Perspective." *International Journal of Lifelong Education,* 1992, *11* (2), 91–101.

Clifford, G. J., and Guthrie, J. W. *Ed School: A Brief for Professional Education.* Chicago: University of Chicago Press, 1988.

Collins, A., Brown, J. S., and Newman, S. E. "Cognitive Apprenticeship: Teaching the Craft of Reading, Writing, and Mathematics." In L. B. Resnik (ed.), *Knowing, Learning, and Instruction: Essays in Honor of Robert Glaser.* Hillsdale, N.J.: Erlbaum, 1989.

Farquharson, A. "Competencies for Continuing Education in the Professions." *Canadian Journal of University Continuing Education,* 1983, 9 (2), 120–125.

Grimmett, P. P., and MacKinnon, A. M. "Craft Knowledge and the Education of Teachers." In G. Grant (ed.), *Review of Research in Education.* Washington, D.C.: American Educational Research Association, 1992.

Hofstede, G. *Culture's Consequences: International Differences in Work-Related Values.* Newbury Park, Calif.: Sage, 1980.

Hunt, D. E. *Beginning with Ourselves in Theory, Practice, and Human Affairs.* Toronto, Ontario, Canada: Ontario Institute for Studies in Education Press, 1987.

McAlpine, L., Frew, E., and Lucas, M. "Mechanisms for Helping 'Becoming' Practitioners Develop Professionals' Ways of Knowing." In *Professionals' Ways of Knowing and the Implications for CPE.* Preconference Proceedings of the Commission for Continuing Professional Education, American Association for Adult and Continuing Education. Montreal, Quebec, Canada: Commission for Continuing Professional Education, American Association for Adult and Continuing Education, 1991. (ED 339 848)

Nowlen, P. M. *A New Approach to Continuing Education for Business and the Professions.* New York: Macmillan, 1988.

Parochka, J., and Fox, R. D. "Family and Community." In R. D. Fox, P. E. Mazmanian, and R. W. Putnam (eds.), *Changing and Learning in the Lives of Physicians.* New York: Praeger, 1989.

Paul, H. A., and Osborne, C. E. "Relating to Others in the Profession." In R. D. Fox, P. E. Mazmanian, and R. W. Putnam (eds.), *Changing and Learning in the Lives of Physicians.* New York: Praeger, 1989.

Resnik, L. B. "Learning in School and Out." *Educational Researcher,* 1987, 16, 13–20.

Schön, D. A. *The Reflective Practitioner: How Professionals Think in Action.* New York: Basic Books, 1983.

Schön, D. A. *Educating the Reflective Practitioner: Toward a New Design for Teaching and Learning in the Professions.* San Francisco: Jossey-Bass, 1987.

Yakowicz, W. J. "Coaching: Collegial Learning in Schools." In V. J. Marsick (ed.), *Learning in the Workplace.* London, England: Croom-Helm, 1987.

H. K. MORRIS BASKETT is professor and program director, Faculty of Continuing Education, University of Calgary, Alberta, Canada.

VICTORIA J. MARSICK is associate professor of adult and continuing education at Teachers College, Columbia University in New York City. She currently consults with both the private and public sectors on the design of learning organizations and training approaches.

RONALD M. CERVERO is associate professor in the Department of Adult Education, University of Georgia, Athens. He is the author of Effective Continuing Education for Professionals *(Jossey-Bass, 1988), winner of the American Association for Adult and Continuing Education's 1989 Cyril O. Houle Award for Literature in Adult Education.*

INDEX

Abbott, A., 114
Abrahamsson, K., 101
Abramowitz, A., 24
Action learning, 104
Adamson, T. E., 32
Adler, N. J., 105
Africa, 101
Allan, D. M., 36
Allery, L. A., 106
American Board of Family Practice, 34
American College of Obstetricians and Gynecologists, 34
American College of Physicians Self-Assessment Program, 34
American Dietetic Association, 26
American Institute of Architects (AIA), self-assessment system of, 19–25
American Medical Association, 34
Architects, self-assessment system for, 19–25
Argyris, C., 9, 62, 104
Articulation, 43, 92
Authentic knowing, 81–85
Azzaretto, J. F., 13

Balint, M., 77
Baskett, H.K.M., 6, 7, 10, 11, 12, 15, 109, 118
Belenky, M. F., 2, 79, 80, 81, 82
Bellah, R. N., 105
Benner, P., 10, 92, 94, 112
Bennett, B., 104
Benveniste, G., 10, 14
Bershad, C., 4, 17, 27, 115
Berwick, D. M., 37
Bole, G. G., 32, 33
Bootstrapping, 47
Boreham, N. C., 4–5, 71, 78, 111
Boshvizen, H.P.A., 98
Boud, D., 9, 11
Broadbent, D. E., 72, 74, 75, 76
Brown, J. S., 41, 42, 114
Buckmaster, A., 4, 5, 41, 42, 49, 114
Bunnell, K. P., 33
Burgoyne, J. G., 9

Caffarella, R. S., 106
Calderhead, J., 10, 117

Campbell, L., 6
Canadian Council on Health Facilities Accreditation, 31
Candy, P. C., 106
Capability development, 4, 54; with cooperative, 56–57; and learning, 57–58; lessons from, 58; strategy for, 54–56
Carnevale, A., 61
Cederholm, L., 56, 104
Cell, E., 82
Cervero, R. M., 5, 13, 29, 36, 47, 101, 103, 109, 113, 114, 118
Chi, M.T.H., 98
Chodorow, N., 85
Clifford, G. J., 113
Clinchy, B. M., 2, 79, 80, 81, 82,
Clinical supervision, 103–104
Clyne, M. B., 77
Cognitive apprenticeship, 4, 41–42, 47–48; effectiveness of, 46–47; example of, 43–44; implementing, 44–46; phases of, 42–43
College of Family Physicians of Canada, 34
Collins, A., 41, 42, 114
Colorado Personalized Education for Physicians Program, 33
Conrath, D., 30
Context, 9–10, 97–98, 115–116; opportunity system as, 105–106; organizational setting as, 102–105; political and economic, 99–100; technological, 101–102
Continuing medical education (CME), 33, 34
Continuing professional education (CPE), 1; cognitive apprenticeship in, 41–48; forces against change in, 116–117; impact of, 12–13; individual learning contracts in, 33–34; and models of women's learning, 85–87; polar issues in, 109–110; peer-based learning in, 31–32; practice-based education in, 33, 38; self-assessment in, 17–26, 34–35; societal influences on, 97–107; suggestions for, 110–116; and technol-

119

Ordering Information

NEW DIRECTIONS FOR ADULT AND CONTINUING EDUCATION is a series of paperback books that explores issues of common interest to instructors, administrators, counselors, and policy makers in a broad range of adult and continuing education settings—such as colleges and universities, extension programs, businesses, the military, prisons, libraries, and museums. Books in the series are published quarterly in fall, winter, spring, and summer and are available for purchase by subscription as well as by single copy.

SUBSCRIPTIONS for 1992 cost $45.00 for individuals (a savings of 20 percent over single-copy prices) and $60.00 for institutions, agencies, and libraries. Please do not send institutional checks for personal subscriptions. Standing orders are accepted.

SINGLE COPIES cost $14.95 when payment accompanies order. (California, New Jersey, New York, and Washington, D.C., residents please include appropriate sales tax.) Billed orders will be charged postage and handling.

DISCOUNTS FOR QUANTITY ORDERS are available. Please write to the address below for information.

ALL ORDERS must include either the name of an individual or an official purchase order number. Please submit your order as follows:
   Subscriptions: specify series and year subscription is to begin
   Single copies: include individual title code (such as CE1)

MAIL ALL ORDERS TO:
   Jossey-Bass Publishers
   350 Sansome Street
   San Francisco, California 94104

FOR SALES OUTSIDE OF THE UNITED STATES CONTACT:
   Maxwell Macmillan International Publishing Group
   866 Third Avenue
   New York, New York 10022

OTHER TITLES AVAILABLE IN THE
NEW DIRECTIONS FOR ADULT AND CONTINUING EDUCATION SERIES
Ralph G. Brockett, Editor-in-Chief
Alan B. Knox, Consulting Editor

U.S. Postal Service

STATEMENT OF OWNERSHIP, MANAGEMENT AND CIRCULATION
Required by 39 U.S.C. 3685

1A. Title of Publication	1B. PUBLICATION NO.	2. Date of Filing
NEW DIRECTIONS FOR ADULT AND CONTINUING EDUCATION	4 9 3 – 9 3 0	10/16/92

3. Frequency of Issue	3A. No. of Issues Published Annually	3B. Annual Subscription Price
Quarterly	Four (4)	$45 (individual) $60 (institutional)

4. Complete Mailing Address of Known Office of Publication *(Street, City, County, State and ZIP+4 Codes) (Not printers)*

350 Sansome Street, San Francisco, CA 94104-1310

5. Complete Mailing Address of the Headquarters of General Business Offices of the Publisher *(Not printer)*

(same address above)

6. Full Names and Complete Mailing Address of Publisher, Editor, and Managing Editor *(This item MUST NOT be blank)*

Publisher *(Name and Complete Mailing Address)*

Jossey-Bass Inc., Publishers (same address above)

Editor *(Name and Complete Mailing Address)*

Ralph G. Brockett, University of Tennessee, 402 Claxton Addition, Knoxville, TN 37996-3400

Managing Editor *(Name and Complete Mailing Address)*

Lynn Luckow, President, Jossey-Bass Inc., Publishers

7. Owner *(If owned by a corporation, its name and address must be stated and also immediately thereunder the names and addresses of stockholders owning or holding 1 percent or more of total amount of stock. If not owned by a corporation, the names and addresses of the individual owners must be given. If owned by a partnership or other unincorporated firm, its name and address, as well as that of each individual must be given. If the publication is published by a nonprofit organization, its name and address must be stated.) (Item must be completed.)*

Full Name	Complete Mailing Address
Maxwell Communications Corp., plc	Headington Hill Hall Oxford OX30BW U.K.

8. Known Bondholders, Mortgagees, and Other Security Holders Owning or Holding 1 Percent or More of Total Amount of Bonds, Mortgages or Other Securities *(If there are none, so state)*

Full Name	Complete Mailing Address
same as above	same as above

9. For Completion by Nonprofit Organizations Authorized To Mail at Special Rates *(DMM Section 423.12 only)*
The purpose, function, and nonprofit status of this organization and the exempt status for Federal income tax purposes *(Check one)*

(1) ☐ Has Not Changed During Preceding 12 Months	(2) ☐ Has Changed During Preceding 12 Months	*(If changed, publisher must submit explanation of change with this statement.)*

10. Extent and Nature of Circulation *(See instructions on reverse side)*	Average No. Copies Each Issue During Preceding 12 Months	Actual No. Copies of Single Issue Published Nearest to Filing Date
A. Total No. Copies *(Net Press Run)*	1400	1421
B. Paid and/or Requested Circulation 1. Sales through dealers and carriers, street vendors and counter sales	94	74
2. Mail Subscription *(Paid and/or requested)*	757	765
C. Total Paid and/or Requested Circulation *(Sum of 10B1 and 10B2)*	851	839
D. Free Distribution by Mail, Carrier or Other Means Samples, Complimentary, and Other Free Copies	62	69
E. Total Distribution *(Sum of C and D)*	913	908
F. Copies Not Distributed 1. Office use, left over, unaccounted, spoiled after printing	487	513
2. Return from News Agents	–0–	–0–
G. TOTAL *(Sum of E, F1 and 2—should equal net press run shown in A)*	1400	1421

11. I certify that the statements made by me above are correct and complete	Signature and Title of Editor, Publisher, Business Manager, or Owner	Larry Ishii Vice-President

PS Form 3526, Feb. 1989 *(See instructions on reverse)*